Shadbolts   10/30/13
                  $15 -

Read 3/17

P9-CSW-544

...but God!

Nancy Sheldon

Nancy Sheldon

Copyright © 2013 Nancy Sheldon

All rights reserved.

ISBN: 1489570276
ISBN-13: 978-1489570277

...but God!

Table of Contents

Forward…

I've know Nancy on different levels for about 17 years. Reading her book has really been a blessing for me. Reading about her adventures has also been a thrilling experience for me. As a fellow missionary, I cried as she shared her heart and I can relate to her views on being a missionary. This book is not just about Guatemala. It's about the call, the answer and counting the cost. It's all good in Him.

Myra Smith
Watchman on the Wall Ministry
Missionary in Guatemala

I met Nancy in 2003 when I participated in my first-ever short-term mission trip. I was humbled and amazed at the work she was doing with the people in that region of Guatemala. I immediately fell in love with the people there and felt the desire to continue to be involved in Nancy's ministry. As of now, I have been down there eight times and each time I am blessed to be a part of the amazing things God is doing in that part of Guatemala. I have personally observed some of the types of happenings Nancy described in this book and really enjoyed reading about her experiences, especially the early days. Even though I wasn't there during those times, her stories make those episodes come to life and demonstrate what a person can accomplish with faith and perseverance.

Jim Day
Abilene, TX
Webmaster for Servant Ministries

Nancy's story is a testament to what God can do with one ordinary woman who is willing to be used for extraordinary results! I led the initial mission trip to Jamaica that changed her life, and have been to Guatemala 10 times. I have known Nancy as a single mom from Michigan, and now the head of a far-reaching ministry in Guatemala. Her faithfulness and commitment to God's call on her life is remarkable, and the Chortí Indians in particular have benefited greatly. Continue to dream big Nancy, as you impact Guatemala for Christ!

Rev. Dr. Thomas Seppo
Director of Operation Transformation
Port Huron, MI

I have been privileged to know Nancy for almost 20 years. We have had some great adventures together, a few of them mentioned in this book. I know Nancy to be tenacious and God loving all at the same time. Her fervor for the Lord and for the Guatemalan people is insurmountable! Not only does she live what she teaches, she exhorts others on a daily basis to live for Jesus and to pursue Him. Her life is a great example of spirit-filled faith and perseverance that challenges us all to continue in the best that the Father has for each of our lives. I can't wait to see what the Lord does through her next!

Rev. Nita Leckenby
Director of Children's Conferences International
Levelland, TX

Wow, what can I say? I am Nancy's sister and I heard firsthand about all of these adventures and was actually a part of a couple of them. She is a great example of what God can do in and through an ordinary person who is sold out for the Kingdom. As I read the book and relived her journey, it amazed me once again the depth of her love and commitment for both God and for the people of Guatemala. You will be amazed, you will laugh, you will cry, you will worry, but ultimately, you will celebrate the power of our God and His absolute love and care for us. Enjoy!

Jeanne Hancock
Missionary to Guatemala

Dedication...

I want to dedicate this book to my mom, Lois Strasser. Mom has gone to be with the Lord, but she always told me that I should write a book of all of my experiences on the mission field. She even saved every newsletter, letter or correspondence that she had received over the years and gave them to me in a box to get me started! Mom, I am grateful for what both you and Dad taught me and for the Bible based principles that you raised me on. I have been able to take that foundation and go further and deeper than I could have ever imagined in having a powerful personal intimate relationship with the Lord.

I dedicate this book also to my children, Hank and Julie. Without the interest that you both showed in going on that first short-term mission trip with the youth back in 1988, I wouldn't have ever stepped out to become involved in missions. You have both grown into fine adults and I am proud of both of you. I pray that this book serves as a legacy to reaffirm so much of what the Lord has done in my life. I pray that it serves as a springboard for both of you to keep your hearts totally committed to the Lord. I believe that you will both do great things for Him in your lives as well!

And I dedicate this book to my first and only (at this time) grandbaby, Eliana. Eliana, I waited for you for a very long time.

You are still a baby at this time, but I pray that you will grow strong and healthy, both physically and spiritually. I pray that at a very tender age you will know and understand Jesus' love for you, the special plan that He has for your life and that you fulfill it completely. I pray that you have a heart and passion for people and for missions and that you allow the Lord to use you to do amazing things!

Preface

The Lord has done some amazing things in my life. My intent is to document some of them so that they may serve as encouragement, challenge and comfort to others who are facing similar things in their lives, or that need a little push to take that step of faith to experience all that God has for them. I have decided to write this book in the format of a series of short stories and individual events or testimonies. They are not going to be in exact chronological order, but when dates are mentioned, they are to the best of my recollection. At the writing of this book, I have been in the mission field for 24 years and so there is a lot to reflect back over. Some of these stories will make you laugh, some may make you cry and some will hopefully cause you to do some soul felt reflection over what they may want to speak into your own life. I invite you to take this journey together with me; to see the amazing things that God has done in my heart and life.

Nancy Sheldon

Getting Started

(1989)

1

You're Going Where?

This was what I heard over the phone as I informed my mom of the decision that I had made to go to the mission field! She said "You have two children."   I answered "Yes I know, they are going with me!"   That was the beginning of our adventure back in the fall of 1988, as we began to make preparation to leave for a one year commitment that was made by me and my children. My children and I had gone on our first time short term mission trip to Jamaica as a youth outreach from our church and me participating as a chaperone. I had no idea of how that trip would impact me and the wheels that it would set into motion. I was a single mom, raising my children since they were very young. I was a secretary at my home church, Life of Faith Fellowship, and oversaw the children's ministry at the church. All considered, I was quite happy and comfortable in *my life*. My willingness to go on that first mission trip in the summer of 1988 was based on *being helpful in any way I could for the 10 day trip* and praying desperately that the Lord would use it to impact my children! …….but God had other ideas. That life changing trip began a chain of events that I would not change for all the world. It wasn't my plan of how my life would be**…..but God!**

2

A Child Shall Lead Them

Isaiah 11:6b "...and a little child will lead them." (Well, maybe not so little)

My 15 year old son, Hank, came home from the church youth group with a comment, ***"There is a short term missions trip that they are going to take the youth on; I would like to go."*** Never in my wildest dreams did I realize what that seed planted in my son's heart would do to change all of our lives. My daughter, Julie, was 12 at the time and she said that she would like to go too. Since the age requirement to participate in this trip to Jamaica was 15, or going into high school, I thought that if I volunteered to go as a chaperone that they would allow me to take my daughter along as well. And that was exactly what happened! It wasn't easy to cover the financial responsibility for the three of us to go! We sold candy, participated in fundraiser dinners, car washes and everything else that was offered plus a few creative ideas of our own, but we raised the required $1800.

I was praying up a storm, asking the Lord to really use this trip to touch my children, to impact them, to cause them to have a deeper spiritual walk in their lives with Him. It was one of the times that I felt that God had shown me His sense of humor. I was rushing heaven's gates to pray for my children's experience and had no clue how this short term trip would impact my own life. I thought that I was going along to oversee the youth and be helpful and assist where I could for 10 days, and then get back to *my life*.

Those 10 days gave me my first *face-to-face* with true poverty and impacted my life to its very core. I remember the last night that we shared as a group, giving each youth and leader the opportunity to share something special that they had experienced; something that they had gleaned from the trip, how they had been impacted or something the Lord had shown them. I remember when it was my turn that I said "I know that we are getting on a plane tomorrow and going home, but there is something in my heart that is saying that this is not the end but rather a new beginning." I did not realize just how prophetic those words were or what they would mean in the future.

A simple comment or incident can change our lives. Sometimes what could be a life changing event or moment, at the time, seems insignificant. That simple comment by my son seemed like a nice gesture or desire on his part but none of us knew what it really meant in the long term. Who put that desire in his heart? Did my son realize how it would affect his life down the road? Did my daughter realize how her interest shown in doing this 10 day trip would affect her life? I was at a major curve in the road and the Lord wanted to put me on a new path and it all started with a simple comment. Lord, help us to really discern and see the importance of the *little things* in our lives that You are trying to use. A single decision made at a crossroads in life can have enormous impact on the direction of our lives and have much greater long-term affect than we can ever imagine!

3

Prayer and Preparation

Learning to follow the Lord's guidance in our lives is a walk of faith. It doesn't usually happen in our timing or the way that we think we want. I have told the Lord on multiple occasions that if He would just send me a fax or written document giving me His plan that I would try to implement it. He apparently has other means in mind to show me His guidance! They usually involve just seeing a small piece of the road in front of me and awaiting my completion of whatever He is showing me before more is revealed.

I had been overseeing the children's ministry at my church for over seven years. What started as the responsibility to make sure that a physical teacher was present for every class and buying cookies on a monthly basis grew into something much bigger. We now had annual summer day camps out at my house in Jeddo for 100-150 children and annual Kids for Jesus events where we invited 700 churches to participate plus quite elaborate Christmas productions, amongst other things. Many people do not enjoy working with kids. I loved it! Working with children, who are always free to show their emotions and give you a hug or a show of their affection, filled a place in my heart as I was in a time of separation in my marriage. It filled that void and God used it as a passion to fill my life for that season. My children were in this age group and so it was something that I could be involved in, in their lives too. I helped to train up other children's workers and we attended some good training seminars to help us develop our children's outreach and learn to use other resources and means to work with the children.

My plate was pretty full and I was beginning to feel the weight of it. Between a full time job at the church and being a single mom plus my work with children's ministry, I at times felt overwhelmed. I sensed a need to step down from children's church, but I resisted it because it was something I truly enjoyed. It all culminated one morning when I finally broke down over a very insignificant issue. We couldn't find my daughter's socks and it was time to leave for school. It was the straw that broke the camel's back and brought me to the realization that I needed to heed what the Lord had been showing me.

I went to my pastor and shared my heart with him. He agreed to put Dave and Nancy as the leaders over the children's ministry. Dave and Nancy had worked with me for many years and were more than prepared to take over. I was to stay on, in an advisory capacity for them for a year, to help them with the transition.

What I felt that the Lord had been telling me was to lay down the children's ministry and to dedicate some quality time to prayer. Now you have to understand that I am *a doer*! I told the Lord, "Okay I will pray, but what can I do?" All I kept hearing was *prayer and preparation*. I kept asking what I needed to prepare for but didn't receive an answer for quite some time. I finally began to rest in my new place and committed myself to the time of prayer and preparation, not understanding what was lying ahead. The best way I know how to describe how I was feeling at that time was that the Lord had taken away my plate of chocolate chip cookies (something I enjoy and these were hot out of the oven too). I needed to let go of that plate without knowing what He would give me new in the future.

It was in that year after I had stepped down from children's ministry that I went on the short term mission trip with my children. This obviously resulted in my feeling called to go into mission work and committing my life in another whole new direction.

The Lord has so much planned for us and usually will not reveal it to us all at once. He is waiting for our trust and confidence to be placed totally in Him. We have to learn how to take those small steps of obedience and the bigger ones too, by faith, without understanding the bigger picture that He has for our lives. Oh but how exciting to learn that He has wonderful things planned for us, if we will just trust Him and follow Him and His guidance.

4

An Anchor of Faith

Once we got back from Jamaica and felt that we were supposed to go to the mission field; one big obstacle stood in our way. That was the sale of our home! According to the divorce settlement I had to be actively trying to sell the home. It had been on the market for four years! It had been listed by realtors in two counties. The realtors would advertise it, have open houses and take all the other measures that are normally taken to promote the sale of a house. We had gotten zero response; no calls, no showings, nothing……it was like the house was invisible. It was a very nice house that we had built ourselves, a 1600 square foot house out in the country on 4.25 acres with a pond, huge machine shed and lots of space. I believe that the Lord gave me those extra four years to raise my children in a house that they had always known as their home.

When it came to taking this step to go to the mission field, a very big step for a single mom with two adolescent children, I used the sale of the house as a *fleece before the Lord* (Biblical example in *Judges 6:36-40*). This was not something that I have done too often in my life, but I wanted God's confirmation to take such a big step, not only for myself but for my children as well. I told the Lord "If you want us to go, then You need to sell this house as a confirmation to us that we are meant to go." He answered in a marvelous way.

After four years of having absolutely no movement on the sale of the house, we currently had it listed just *by owner* and not under a real estate company. There was a sign on the front yard that said "For sale by owner" with a telephone number on it. We lived on a dirt road about a ¼ mile off the main road. On a Sunday afternoon, a family that lived halfway across the state of Michigan; were out on a Sunday afternoon drive. They just happened to go down our road and just happened to be looking to buy a house in the area. They jotted down the number and gave me a call a couple of days later. Less than a week after I had given my prayer fleece to the Lord, I got a call from the family saying that they would like to come see the house. My heart soared and wondered if this was the answer that I had been praying for. A few days later the family came to see the house. They seemed to like it and said that they would be in touch. They called back and asked to talk to me again in person. They were also born-again Christians. My excitement died when they gave me the offer on the house, an amount enormously under the asking price.

I began a dialogue with them, something like: "I have never sold a house before. I don't know how to play the real estate games. We are all Christians. Can we just put our cards on the table and be honest with one another? I feel that the Lord wants me to go to the mission field and I have to sell this house and pay off my mortgage before I can do that. I think that you want to buy this house and I would love to sell it to you, but I cannot give it to you for what you are offering." They asked me, "Nancy, what do you have to get for it?" Again, not playing the *games* but knowing in my heart the bottom line of what I was willing to drop to, I gave them that price. The husband looked at the wife and she looked at him and then they both turned to look at me! They said "Nancy, when we prayed, that was the exact price that we felt that the Lord gave us; we were just trying to get it for less! We feel that this is the Lord directing us all. We will cover all closing costs and legal fees (normally divided between seller and buyer); we will make sure that when you leave the bank that you will have that amount to the penny!"

God used that incident in so many ways. It gave me the peace and confidence to move forward to take this huge step that I had in my heart. It served as an anchor so many times, especially during those first several months, to remind me that *this was what I was supposed to be doing.* When I got frustrated with not knowing the language well, when I missed my culture and ability to do things as I had always done them, when doubt crowded in and I would cry out "Lord, are you sure?", it was the anchor that held me fast and always brought me back to knowing how God had confirmed this step of faith in my life. I have thanked Him many times for giving me such a tangible event that I could hold on to when I sometimes questioned what we were doing. Thank God I held fast to that anchor of knowing that we were in the right place!

5

Why There?

A lot of people over the years have asked me the question "Why There? Why Guatemala, why that part of Guatemala? How did you find it?" When I made the decision to go to the mission field, my pastor wanted to try to help me plug into a ministry that the church was connected with. We sent out feelers to three places that the church supported through their missions outreach; Peru, Africa and Guatemala. The door seemed to open for Guatemala. There was a couple, Bob and Barb Cook; that had previously worked in Colombia but later started working in Guatemala. They, along with other North Americans had helped to start a Bible Institute in Guatemala City. They felt the Lord was calling them to leave the city and to start a pioneer work in an untouched area. A study was done of all of the different parts of Guatemala and all of the different Mayan tribes. There are approximately 30 different Mayan tribes in Guatemala! The Chortí, a smaller Mayan group, was considered to be the least reached with the Gospel. They were also considered to be amongst the poorest and neediest. When I went for my visit to Guatemala to check it out and decide whether I would go there, we made a day trip to Jocotán. Jocotán is a small town in the eastern region of Guatemala in the department (county) of Chiquimula. A decision was made to begin a work there. Bob and Barb Cook moved to Jocotán in January 1989 and I arrived with my children the following month.

6

Guatemala or Bust – "Beverly Hillbillies" Style

On February 5, 1989 we pulled out of the church parking lot after that Sunday morning service. But it wasn't like every other Sunday, where we had a 30 minute drive to go *home*. Our house had been sold and we were driving to Guatemala. We had made a one year commitment to go work with a family that was already established there. We had made a decision, as a family, to give a year of our lives to do something similar to what we had experienced on our short term trip to Jamaica......to reach out and be used to minister to those in need.

I have often thought that the scripture *1 Corinthians 1:27 "But God chose the foolish things of the world to shame the wise, God chose the weak things of the world to shame the strong"* was a great description of us as we pulled out that day. There was a little bit of snow on the ground. We had 3500 miles to drive, with a double axel horse trailer pulled behind our little 4 cylinder 4x4 jeep. My son was 15, with a learner's permit to drive! He would be my only relief driver on this long excursion. Neither of us knew how to back up the trailer and we did not learn during the trip. We had to be very careful where we pulled in; making sure that we could pull out without having to back up! There was a spiritual lesson here, of moving forward and not looking back! The Lord had a new chapter in our lives and we were just faith-filled enough and maybe a little bit crazy☺, to step out and see what the Lord wanted to do.

We had 25 year old appliances in our trailer that someone from the church had donated. We had everything pretty much that we would need to be away for a year. What do you take when you don't know what kind of food you will be able to buy? For us, it included 35 pounds of peanut butter (good choice, we couldn't get that) and 50 pounds of popcorn (that we did find, but what can I say, we like popcorn). We had our two family dogs with us, which made the trip that much more interesting.

The trip took nine days of driving 12 hours a day. We met a Canadian couple in Houston, Texas who also had given a one year commitment to work with the same ministry in Guatemala. We crossed the Mexican border and completed the journey together; kind of like the blind leading the blind. With my one semester of Spanish under my belt, I was sadly the most proficient in getting us through the borders and other communication.

What laid ahead? What would be our experience? How would the Lord use this time? We had no idea; but we stepped out in faith to find out!

February 5, 1989. The adventure begins!
The day we left church to drive to Guatemala.

7

If You Come Back, We Will Kill You!

We visited the village of Oquen and the ministry families (four of us at that time) decided that this would be a good area to begin to open up to the Gospel. It was in a remote area and at that time did not have a road that went all the way to it. We could drive half way and then had to walk another hour by foot. On our first visit, we went to just get the feel for the area. Our greeting was *"If you come back, we will kill you!"* We were the first white people that they had seen and having light hair and blue eyes just added to our mystery to the people. There was only one other North American family that lived in town and they were Bible translators and had spent time in another village but spent most of their time translating, as was their job.

I had brought my children to this environment and had to wonder whether we were all crazy. But people are always going to react to what they don't understand! It was the fear speaking through the people and the answer was to develop a relationship of trust with them and to show them that we were there to help not to bring harm to anyone. My children and I, along with Tom (the man, along with his family, who had accompanied us on our drive to Guatemala) went to this village twice a week. It is where we built our first church in 1990, about a year later.

Our walking trip to Oquen, 1989

8

Motorcycle Guides

When we first arrived in Guatemala, we had to stay in the capital for a couple of weeks. There was paperwork to get done for my vehicle, there was immigration work to be done and we were trying to get ready to move to Jocotán; where we would live. Guatemala City at that time had a population of about 2 million people. If you have never driven in a Latin country, you don't know what you are missing. People make their own lanes, cut in front of you, and eternity to them is the time it takes you to take your foot off the brake and start to accelerate when the traffic light turns green. No turn signals were used and you had to have a passenger to do *hand waving* to indicate that you wanted to change lanes. Then you add just the chaos of having a city of 2 million people and everyone using their horns. It was very intimidating…..especially to someone who had lived in a quiet small country town for 20 years prior to this new adventure.

I had paperwork to get done and would get so frustrated at getting lost, trying to get someone to get me back on track, just to get lost again; with the need to keep moving because everyone was honking at me. I'd pull out my map and show where I was trying to go and it seemed like the first words out of everyone's mouth was "It's easy, you just….." My last attempt to ask for directions was from a young man on a motorcycle. He must have seen how frustrated I was and took pity on me because he actually offered to guide me to the place I was looking for. It was awesome! I then asked him what he was doing for the rest of the afternoon and asked him if he would help me finish my other errands, which he did. He wound up going back to the house we were staying at, and helped to hook up our horse trailer so that we could make the 4-5 hour drive to Jocotán. He actually led us to the edge of the city and put us on the right highway to get us to where we were going. I stopped to profusely thank him for his assistance and tried to give him some money. He refused it and said that he was happy to help.....the guy had spent 3-4 hours of his day helping a stranger! I told him to PLEASE take my token of gratitude and to again let him know how much of a help he had been. It was a standing joke with the other missionaries in the future that I had learned my way around the capital well enough so that I didn't have to hire any more motorcycle drivers! Don't you know that the young man really had a story to tell when he got home for dinner that night and told about the crazy gringa (what they call North Americans) lady that he had been guiding around town!

9

How Long will it Take?

We had been in Guatemala for about six weeks. The head missionary, Bob, came to me and told me that they wanted to go to a mountain village where Christians had never been. The village was called Oregano. He wanted me to go along, but I think more than anything he needed my vehicle to help transport people. I found out that it was me and 8-9 men that would be going; some North Americans and some Guatemalans. I understood that we had to drive for about an hour and a half and then we had to walk. I asked "How long will it take to walk?" After a pause I got the answer "a couple of hours". Now I had been a church secretary prior to going to the mission field, meaning that I did a lot of sitting and was overweight to boot so I was definitely concerned about my stamina; especially in the heat of what was the hottest time of the year.

We drove our hour and a half and parked the vehicles. I was armed with a backpack that included some drinking water, Bible, candy and balloons to hand out to kids, bug spray etc. The first part of our *walk* was following a railroad track which wasn't bad. Then we got to a long tunnel. It was totally black inside and you had to walk in-between the tracks and hold on to the shoulder of the person in front of you. No one had thought to bring a flashlight for a morning excursion. As we came to the other end of the tunnel and you could begin to see something, there were hundreds of bats flying around and squealing, but there was no choice but to move forward. We came to a place where we had to leave the railroad tracks after an hour, and then the walking got much harder. We were on very rough cut trails and going up and down ravines and climbing over fences and logs and had to cross a river. At about two hours I asked "How much further?" Then it comes out that no one had actually been to this village and they weren't sure how much further it was!!!! We pushed on and the climbs became steeper. It was all I could do to put one foot in front of the other. I had to stop frequently to rest as I was getting very winded and my leg muscles felt like jelly and that someone had taken out my bones. I felt like I could just fall down like a pool of Jello. I know I am showing just how soft I was but I had never in my life had to exert myself to that point. We had been walking for four hours when we finally reached the village. I sat down in the dirt and cried and had my pity party with God; asking Him what the purpose in all of this was and many other questions I had for Him at the moment. The men left me to go door-to-door. There was a centralized area with houses and we found out later a school, which is not the norm for mountain villages. After I had been sitting awhile, I began to hear children's voices. I thought it was a school and made myself get up to go investigate. It was indeed a school and I thought that the teacher was telling me that yes I could hand out the candy and balloons and share with the children too if I wanted. While I was trying to figure out everything the teacher had been saying, Bob and the other men came back and he confirmed that the teacher was giving me a chance to talk to the children. He said "Nancy, share your testimony with them." He said that he would help to translate when I couldn't say things in Spanish. So that is what I did. I at least was beginning to see *some reason* for the self-torture that I had inflicted upon myself in getting to this very remote area.

Now the realization soon came to me that we still had to go down the mountain and I just didn't know where I would find the strength to do that. One of the Guatemalan men that was with us pulled out some bread from his bag and loaded it up with a huge amount of mango jelly and gave it to me. He told me that the sugar would give me energy. Everyone told me to just take my time and not to rush. Now if you have never done much mountain walking, you may think that going downhill should have been much easier. For the Guatemalans that are used to doing these trails, they skip along and just make it look easy. But for someone that is trying to do it slow and realizing the need to have strength in your legs to brake, it is another story. I made it about 10-15 minutes down the trail. I came to a sharp turn where I should have stayed on the trail but got caught up in some loose rocks and my feet went out from under me. Instead of taking the turn I went off the trail and was somersaulting down the mountain. I had a skirt on because especially back then we would never think of wearing pants, so I got very scratched up as I fell. The only things to grab to try to stop myself were thorn bushes. The North American guys were ahead of me but some of the Guatemalans had seen me fall and scampered down the side of the mountain to see how I was. It took three of them to get me back up to the trail. They tried to ask me if I was hurt and I indicated that one ankle/foot was really hurting plus being covered by thorns that had penetrated my hands, legs and arms. Nicolas, a pastor, just happened to have some medical alcohol which he pulled out and administered to my arms and legs, not a pleasant experience. They indicated that I should take off my shoe, but I told them I didn't think that was a good idea. They cut me some crutches out of sticks and indicated that I was going to have to walk down the mountain! It was pure torture! I knew that it was my foot that was hurting and going downhill put all of the weight on my toes. The Guatemalans were very gracious and stayed with me as I slowly made my way down the mountain. When we got to the river, I just sat down in it and cried but the cold water felt good and I wasn't concerned about my clothes getting wet. We eventually made it down the mountain and back to my vehicle, which someone else had to drive for me. When I got home, I realized just how much grace God had given me to get off of that mountain. I tried to step out of the car and my foot was done and would not allow me to support myself.

I was put to bed and some of the missionaries came to see how I was doing. The head missionaries, Bob and Barb, came more equipped to deal with the situation. Because they didn't know if these thorns were poisonous, they were very concerned to get them out of me. Without anything to deaden the pain, they began a very long process of digging all of these thorns out of my body which took a very long time, one holding a light and one digging with a scalpel. Bob told me after it was over, "Nancy, if this doesn't send you home, I am convinced that you are called!" I found out that I had 3 broken toes and my foot ranged in color from black to purple to red to green and yellow. I really thought that my foot was broken because it took a very long time to heal. We had an x-ray taken later. They told me that besides my broken toes that my foot was extremely bruised and that it would just take time to mend. It has been an ongoing prayer to the Lord to ask Him that if *anyone was affected by our trip to Oregano, if anyone became a believer as a result of the seeds that we planted* that I wanted to know when I got to heaven and have a chance to meet them.

Our trip to Oregano.

10
We Aren't Cannibals!

In those early days of opening up our first village in Oquen, we learned that the people were very superstitious and for the most part uneducated and illiterate. All of this adds more challenges when trying to reach a people group with the Gospel. They had many beliefs built on nothing but silly folklore and passed on stories. Without the ability to read the Bible for themselves, we too were asking them to believe something based on what we told them but trying to show them the difference of it being based on the truth of the Word of God. We were still trying to win their trust and did what we could to reach out to their natural needs as well as their spiritual needs. We received a donation of Gerber baby food from Operation Blessing through the 700 Club. Although baby food, it was nourishment for people of any age, especially when you are hungry. So we began to pass it out.

Now, when you buy a can of tomato paste, it many times has a picture of a tomato on the front or an apple is shown on the can of apple juice you may buy etc. What is on the front of a bottle of Gerber baby food? Right, a baby! The people thought that we were giving them ground up babies to eat!!!!! They said we must be cannibals! We had to explain that it was food for babies but that it would fill their stomachs and not hurt them.

They finally believed us and left with their baby food to carry it home with them.

11

Why Don't You Want Me in Guatemala?

When you arrive in Guatemala, you receive a 90 day tourist visa or permission to be in the country. In the early days, that was the only status I had. Every 90 days I had to leave the country for a couple of days and then re-enter. I will never forget the first time that I attempted this procedure.

Thankfully the Honduras border was only an hour away, down a pot holed dirt road, but at least it wasn't too far. Between the Guatemalan side and the Honduran side, there were 13 offices that you had to go through. Each office gave you a stamp on a piece of paper that they issued you and each office collected something. There was a town an hour into Honduras so I stayed at a hotel there.

I was allowed to re-enter Guatemala on the third day. When I was back on the Guatemalan side of the offices, they asked me what my profession was. I thought, okay I can handle this one. When my reply brought a gasp out of them and they didn't seem to want to stamp my passport to allow me to enter, I became concerned. Someone, through a mixture of talking and playing charades, made me to understand that I had just told them that "I was a teacher and a mercenary!" I obviously understood their distress and assured them that I had been trying to say that I was a missionary! Learning a language provides lots of stories to tell with all of the mistakes that you are bound to make! Success only comes as you learn to laugh at your mistakes and keep moving forward to perfect your language skills.

My second trip back from Honduras wasn't much better. I had heard of a goat program in Honduras and wanted to find out if it would be difficult to bring animals across the border. Just to have the information, I tried to inquire about this. When they asked me what kind of animal I wanted to bring into Guatemala, I made another error. I said "cobra" instead of "cabra". I asked to bring cobras into Guatemala and told them it was for the milk that they could provide. After confused looks and some more attempts to explain "a goat", we got it clear. It was only one letter different after all, but what a difference that one letter can make!

12

You Have 48 Hours to Leave the Country

I only had one semester of Spanish when I went to live in Guatemala. Not knowing the language can make life challenging and one of the areas that is most difficult is with your paperwork. Back when I came to Guatemala, there were no phones in our area. The only means of communication were telegrams. I felt like I was stepping back in time. In those early months I received a telegram from the immigration office telling me that I had 48 hours to leave the country. I had no idea why. It was a 4-5 hour drive to the capital to go to the immigration office. It looked like a huge bank with all kinds of windows. It took awhile to figure out which window I should be at. The woman at the window read my telegram, reiterated some long explanation to me and then just stared at me. I told her I didn't understand. She repeated her long dissertation. It didn't help, I still didn't understand. After that, she just waved me off with her hand. I felt very helpless.

I went to a church that I knew in the capital and they hooked me up with a lawyer from their church who spoke some English. He explained what I had to do to resolve the issue and offered to help me. It was taken care of but it was only the beginning of so much more paperwork that I would have to deal with in the future. It took 16 years to finally have the permanent residency status that I now have. People don't realize how difficult and time consuming all of this paperwork can be. It is a good area to pray for when you pray for missionaries; for favor with the government, authorities, with their paperwork and for the right people to be in place to help get the job done.

13

Supernatural Touch on the Children

We had set up a tent in the village of Escobillal. This was in 1989 and we were trying to open up our first village in Oquen. Because we couldn't drive all of the way to Oquen, we had set up the tent in Escobillal, which was as close as we could get. We were having a 3-day evangelistic crusade. We always had a class for the children before we had the main service for the adults. Lots of children attended. We had given a teaching to them about the "Baptism of the Holy Spirit" and then gave an invitation for them to respond. There were many that came forward but there were 6-7 children that got an extra special touch. As we prayed for them, they automatically began to speak in tongues, even though we hadn't really talked about that with the children too much. Their hands were raised to heaven and they continued on in their God given prayer language! God was definitely doing something but we didn't know what to do. We had another 150 children that were in the chairs and waiting for the movie to be shown. We concluded each day with a movie for the children and it was a highlight for them. None of these children had a television or even electricity in their homes, so seeing a movie was a huge deal! We finally started up the movie and just left the children up front, to allow God to finish whatever He was doing. Those children went on for 45 minutes, with their hands never coming down and praying in their heavenly language! I would have loved to have seen what may have been going on in their minds or hearts, because something was definitely happening!

I worked with children before going to the mission field and they still have a special place in my heart. In the early days in Guatemala, the Guatemalan churches didn't put much focus on their children. I am thankful to say that that has changed a lot over the years. There is a story that I have told many times in the churches here, to get across a point.

An evangelist had just finished giving a 3-day evangelistic crusade and was talking to his friend about it. The friend asked if it had been a good crusade and if there had been any fruit, any souls given to the Lord. The evangelist answered that there had been 7 ½ souls given to the Lord. The friend was confused and asked how 7 ½ people could give their lives to God. Then he thought he had come up with the solution and said "Oh I know, it was seven adults and a child (the child being counted as half)!" The evangelist replied "No, it was seven children and one adult. The adult only has half of his life to give to God. The children still have their whole lives to offer!"

There is a real lesson in this story and one I have shared many times in Guatemala. Babies have a need for nourishment from the time they are born. The food may be different and come from a different form of preparation, but it is necessary from the beginning of life. Children have the same need for spiritual food and teaching as well. The *food* may need to be prepared differently and portion sizes may vary, but they have the very real need to learn about God. I was 25 before I gave my life over to the Lord in a personal relationship. How wonderful for children to learn from a very tender age of their need and to respond to that need as these children in this tent meeting did.

Tent crusade in Escobillas 1989

Tent meeting.

14

You Haven't Called Me to Have my Children Suffer

We were renting a house in the town of Jocotán. Back in 1989 there were few conveniences available to us. We had to drive 8-9 hours round trip once a month to do a real grocery shopping in anything that resembled a store more modern than Sam Drucker's store in Petticoat Junction. We received telegrams as a means of communication, had to drive over an hour to rent the closest phone and it took a two month turnaround time to send and receive a snail mail letter....IF they arrived at all!

Along with our rustic living, there was no other option for my children's education other than *home schooling*. My kids had been attending a Christian school back in Michigan and the school was good enough to allow them to stay registered under it as we moved to Guatemala. Home schooling was not all that popular back then and I knew that my son had expressed his desire to go to college and I didn't want to do anything that would cause him a problem to fulfill that goal. When we arrived in Guatemala Hank was half way through 10th grade and Julie was halfway through 7th. I was their teacher! Even 7th grade grammar was a bit of a challenge; as you had to diagram sentences etc. and I had been out of school for a long time! I also gave a Spanish class to them and it gave them credit toward taking a foreign language. Living in a country where they *had to learn* the language definitely gave them the opportunity to learn so much more than what they ever would have by taking a foreign language back in the United States. When I got to the point with my son getting into pre-trigonometry and pre-calculus I knew I was in trouble! I had been a good student and graduated from high school in the top 10% of my graduating class of almost 1000 students, but I only went as far as geometry.

I really began to pray. I didn't know how to help my son. We were living in a third world country where the majority of the people were not educated back then, many did not read (even in town), most did not get beyond basic arithmetic (addition and subtraction) and all of this in their language....certainly not in English! I told the Lord that I didn't believe that He had called me into missions to have my children suffer and that I needed help!

The Lord taught me a great lesson on His provision and how He is not limited by our circumstances or geography. Shortly after me recognizing my need and experiencing my total helplessness to do anything about it, a North American woman knocked on my door. I don't even remember her name but she was an angel sent by God! She told me that she was in the Peace Corps and that she was living in Jocotán. She had heard that another North American family lived there and had come by to meet us. We chatted and in the course of talking she said "I know you must be home schooling. If you need any help, let me know!" I quickly asked her how strong she was in math and whether she could help Hank. She was willing and with just a little bit of help, Hank was on track and did fine.

It was an awesome lesson to me to know that God would send His provision in what seemed a hopeless case....and He brought it right to my front door.

Home Schooling

15

You're Going to Hell Five Times

I often felt like I was stepping back in time, especially in those early years. There were very few conveniences and people had Christian beliefs that mirrored what I had heard from people that were brought up in the old Pentecostal churches back in the 60s in the United States. Everything was a sin! When a visiting pastor asked one time what the biggest sins in town were, this is what the church people answered:

1.   Smoking
2.   Drinking
3.   Playing cards
4.   Pornography

I had an experience early on when a *pastor* came to me and told me that I would go to hell five times. I thought that that was a new doctrine. To go five times, they would have to let you out and let you re-enter; not sure what scripture back up he had for that. My huge offenses to warrant this were:

1.   I had cut my hair in my life time.
2.   I had a ring on.
3.   I wore makeup.
4.   I had clear nail polish on.

5.   I forget the fifth one, but I'm sure it was just as serious.

What was really sad is that this pastor was soon sent to jail for molesting children and he was worried about all of *my offenses*. It is sad to see people get legalistic like this; it's not how God designed it. He looks at our hearts and He changes us from the inside out. We can make all kinds of outward changes but without a true heart change, it really doesn't mean anything. The same changes, when someone is convicted in their heart by God that they need to make the change in a particular area may look the same on the outside but it is totally different. People always confuse religion with relationship. I do not like religion as we see it today. Religion is man's attempt to reach God. Being in personal relationship with the Lord is all about Him reaching out to us and us responding!

When you go to a new culture, you have to sift through what is legalism and what is culture. For example even in recent times, it is rare to see a mountain village woman not wear a dress or skirt. For them, that is just part of their culture and they do not look at pants as being a sin, they just look at them as being men's clothing! So to respect them, I wear a skirt when I go to their village. When they come to my house, they will find me wearing pants or capris. When we have teams come in, we ask them to respect the culture and forget some of their trappings that are perfectly acceptable when they are home. If you want to form a relationship and try to impact someone's life, you have to meet them where they are at and try to figure out the difference of whether it is cultural beliefs, personal preferences or pure legalism.

16

B.Y.O.R. (Bring Your Own Rock)

Here is another story about our beginnings in the village of Oquen. We had spent a number of weeks going hut-to-hut and building relationships with the people and beginning to evangelize. We wanted to start having a joint meeting that we could invite people to attend once a week. For 20 quetzales a month (about $6.50), we rented a dilapidated hut that was made of palm branches that had seen better days and had all kinds of holes in the walls and roof. It had a dirt floor. We told the people that they would have to bring their rock with them to sit on inside of the hut so that they didn't have to stand! This was how we began; by people bringing their own seat to church with them in the form of a rock! But the people came and they brought their rock and this was our humble beginnings!

Our "rented" house in Oquen to have services

17

Culture Shock in Reverse

People usually think of culture shock as something that requires you to adapt to a new place to live. While that is true and very real, it also works in reverse. I remember the first time that I returned to the United States after living in Guatemala for only 4-5 months. I went to stay with my parents for a few days. I remember my mom asking me if I wanted to go to the mall. I looked at her and said, "Mom, just let me turn on the hot water faucet and feel the warm water, let me turn on the light switches to see how much it lights up the room. Maybe in a few days I will be up to going to the mall."

I had been in a place, although not that long, where people didn't know where their next meal was coming from. I came from a place where people had one outfit of clothes to their name and that not in good condition. Many didn't wear shoes. Many were sick. When I got back to the United States, I picked up on things that I had not noticed before. I noticed how much people complained. I heard rude customers demanding that their food be taken back and recooked. I caught comments of people who talked about expensive jewelry, bigger televisions, and newer *whatevers*. Thankfully I had enough wisdom to just ponder upon all of this and store it in my heart, but it grieved me. These people were living the only life that they knew, going on with *business as usual*. I was the one that had changed! It made me see things differently. For the most part I kept quiet but took advantage of when a door opened to share with someone concerning all I had experienced.

Now I have learned that I live in two worlds. Sometimes it takes a day or two after traveling to remind myself of which world I am in and how my conduct has to adapt to those surroundings. I always talk to the teams that come down about the possibility of them experiencing difficulty after they return home. Sometimes a group comes from one church, with their pastor accompanying them. They are experiencing the same thing and so share in the emotions that many times are felt and can identify with one another. But that is not always the case. Sometimes someone hooks up with a team and is coming from a church that is not mission minded at all and there is no support awaiting them when they return home to help them process their emotions. I always tell people to not be afraid of what they are feeling. It is a good thing to feel compassion and love for people, to empathize with their lives. God gave us those emotions and I know that He feels intensely for humanity. Sometimes we have to learn to not let those emotions overwhelm us and consume us. They are the foundation that will spring us forward as we know the heart of God more and see things as He sees them.

I will share an example of what I am saying. Tim came down to Guatemala for a mission trip. He was really touched and impacted by all that he had experienced. When he got home he told his wife and others what an awesome time he had, but tears were frequent and not everyone understood his tears. Shortly after his return, his wife and he were discussing what they wanted for supper and they decided on chili dogs. They jumped in their car and went to the grocery store and picked up what they needed. At the checkout Tim began to hyperventilate and couldn't catch his breath. He handed his wallet to his wife and made a comment about needing to get out of there. His wife paid for the groceries and came out to find her husband at the car and asked him "What is wrong with you?" Tim answered her "You don't understand. We just decide what we want for supper, jump in the car and go get what we need. I just came from a place where people don't always know when their next meal is coming!" Tim had been touched and I praise God for his tender heart to feel and express what he had experienced. God wants us to feel, He gave us our emotions. We just need His help sometimes to know how to process them!

18

A Giving Heart

I will never forget a woman that we referred to as *the little widow lady*! She was about 70 years old and was dying of tuberculosis! She attended our meetings in the village of Escobillal. She gave her heart to the Lord and later was baptized in the Holy Spirit. At her age, when it is hard to make changes to what she had always known, the Lord did a very special work in her heart. This woman was beyond poor. She had one dress to her name. It was green and it had been mended countless times and pulled apart at the seams due to the rotting material. Her name was Felipe. Felipe was raising her granddaughter, as both of her parents had abandoned her at birth. Felipe came to my house in town at least once a week. It took her about an hour to make the walk. She never came to my house empty handed. She always brought me something. It could be two bananas or a turkey egg or three small potatoes, but it was always something! In the beginning, it broke my heart. I didn't want to accept what she brought. I knew that she needed it so much more than I did. Many times she didn't know when her next meal was coming. The Lord quickly showed me that it was important to accept her gifts and that through them that He would bless her! This woman had nothing by the world's standards, but she taught me something about true love and about a giving heart!

Felipe has gone on to be with the Lord. She was not even given a proper burial. She died when I was out of town. She was in a hospital, where her body was burned. I look forward to seeing her again in heaven and to let her know how much she impacted my life!

Felipe

19

Is My Spanish That Bad?

Language learning is a huge part of adapting to another culture where *your language* is not spoken. Remember that I only had one semester of Spanish that I had taken at a junior college before leaving for the mission field. The first village we began to work in, Oquen, brought another challenge because they spoke a Mayan dialect called Chortí. Spanish was our only common ground and it was their second language and I had a long way to go to perfect mine...and my Chortí words could be counted on two hands.

Having been a children's teacher at my home church gave me many ways to share in a way that went beyond just words. One of the tools I used was flannel graph. For the younger generation I will explain that this was a method of using Bible character figures, cut out of flannel, and then put on a board as you told the story. I had been in Guatemala only a matter of months but decided to give my first Bible lesson and I chose the Creation Story.

Now even the best of us gets a little intimidated over learning a language, knowing that we are probably butchering it and making a gazillion mistakes as we try to communicate. But it sure didn't give me confidence when the people began to snicker at my story. I'm thinking I must really be making a lot of mistakes and they don't understand what I am saying. Then I came to a realization. As I am telling the story of creation (mostly reading the account from the Bible) and putting up different animals on my board, I understood that the people had never seen a giraffe or an elephant or the many other animals that exist outside of the farm animals that they knew. When you think about it, a giraffe is a pretty funny looking animal with his long neck or an elephant with an extended trunk. I decided that we had to first have a talk about the different animals before I tried to spiritualize it into a Bible story for them, so we spent the rest of the lesson just talking about the animals which the people enjoyed!

House meeting in Oquen.

20

Praise to the Lord!

I had been going up to Oquen for a few weeks and decided to actually try to witness to someone on our hut-to-hut visitation. Now I want to make clear that I don't consider myself an evangelist in anyway but I know that we are all called to witness. Just to say that it wasn't something that came natural to me. Then you add to it that you are trying to do it in a language that you are in the process of learning and needing to really pick your words. I was sitting on a rock in someone's yard and trying to communicate with them. I got totally distracted when a big turkey came up to me and wrapped his neck around my arm. Now I don't know what that means to a turkey or the reason for the gesture but at least he didn't peck me. He got me off track to say the least. The family finally made a comment "Praise to the Lord" and I perked right up thinking that they must be Christians. Then I discovered that *the Lord* to them was the sun. I found out that their religious beliefs were grounded in animism which is the worship of creation rather than the Creator. The sun was the Lord, the moon was the Queen and if you lived a really good life then one day you got to become a Star. I thought "Lord, I am way over my head! I'm talking about the Son and they are interpreting it as the Sun! Jesus, help!" Well, it certainly helped us to know where the people were coming from and how we had to try to reach them….but I will never forget my first attempt at evangelism in Oquen.

21

Humble Beginnings

In later years people would look at the ministry center that God allowed and helped us to build. But they had no idea of how we began and the process that it took to build that ministry center, some 10 years later. The house we rented in Jocotán originally had one electrical breaker. You had to choose what you could use and what order to use things. The only roof was the corrugated tin that you would see on a barn lean-to and in a climate that buried the highest temperatures on the thermometer; it made for some very hot living. My son, Hank, was known in those beginning days to live in shorts, flip flops and no shirt and went through deodorant tubes right and left, trying to stay ahead of the heat. The water in Jocotán was not drinkable but had to be used for everything else. It came from a stagnate offshoot of the river and was very dirty. The water in the toilet (our gauge to see how the water was each day) went from weak tea to black coffee depending on the rain or other factors.

We had a washing machine but there was no plumbing for it. It sat next to the pila (a laundry wash tank that held a small amount of water) and you had to bail water into it for each wash or rinse cycle. Nothing was grounded so pouring water into a metal washer brought lots of highly exhilarating experiences; some that you felt for hours later.

We went grocery shopping in the capital once a month to do a real shopping; which entailed an eight hour round trip. You learned to make a list or do without! There was no freezer section with processed food; everything had to be made from scratch. Little local stores had very few items to select from. Meat was bought only in an open meat market, which meant having someone hack off a piece of meat from whatever chunk of meat was hanging from a recent butcher and you tried not to think about the flies that covered it. The pigs were slaughtered right around the corner from us and we would awake to the squealing process. My daughter, Julie, was not quite 13 when we moved to Guatemala but to this day she is both a vegetarian and a vegan; I'm sure due in part from her experiences in Guatemala. Thankfully there was a good supply and variety of fresh fruit and vegetables year round, eggs were farm fresh and the chicken was not pumped full of steroids.

Fruit and vegetables had to be washed and soaked in bleach water before consuming them. You just learned to disinfect things before putting them away in the fridge. The refrigerator was out in a back hallway, almost in the back yard, because none of the doors were wide enough to actually put it in the kitchen. We still have to soak our vegetables to disinfect them, but I have learned that a little bit of bleach goes a long ways. In those early days I was so afraid of us getting sick that I went through a lot of bleach and everything tasted like bleach and kept our inside plumbing cleaned out if you know what I mean.

There was no phone of course, that wouldn't come for 14 years when a land line phone became available. The closest available phone was an hour's drive down the mountain at a public phone company where you waited your turn. We made one phone call a month; that lasted about two minutes to find out what the monthly deposit into our bank account was. Phone calls to the United States cost $2-3 per minute when we first started.

Our first Christmas tree consisted of a branch off of a huge pine tree that we put in a tin can and leaned in the corner. It made Charlie Brown's Christmas tree look spectacular. But it was given to us with love from a local pastor, because he knew that we were accustomed to having a Christmas tree. It was a far cry from the elaborate Christmas decorations that we would host in years to come, when we invited the whole town in to view them.

Little by little, we made improvements although it took time because we didn't have any extra support to do such renovations. We got our furniture a little at a time. My son, Hank, didn't have a bed for the first six months. We added electrical plugs, more breakers, a drop ceiling, kitchen cupboards etc, little by little. Our original monthly rent cost $53 per month and that was for a three bedroom house.

The Bible tells us not to despise small beginnings and I found that to be very true. It certainly made our initial acclimation harder but it taught us the lesson of being content with what was available and to depend on the Lord. Things have changed over the years! We now have cell phones and high speed internet available to us. But it wasn't always that way and I remember how it all began!

Our first Christmas tree (branch)

Nancy Sheldon

Photo Gallery

Getting Started

Pastor Emilio in La Puente.

Typical housing.

Home cooked meal.

Side Street in "town"

Typical housing

Our church services are "come as you are"!

Panoramic view of the mountains.

Mountains surrounding Jocotán.

Mountain View

Early Years (1990-1999)

Nancy Sheldon

22

He Will Be a Husband to You

I am single, not by choice, but by circumstance. Or at least that was the result of the breakup of my marriage of 16 years. After my husband left I dedicated my life to being a single mom and raising my children. My life consisted of motherhood, my job at the church, my involvement in the children's ministry at my church and first and foremost my relationship and walk with the Lord. I never dated. I was standing in faith for the restoration of my marriage for eight years after the separation; right up until the divorce was final. In my heart it would have been double minded to do anything else. I still don't have all of the answers and probably never will, this side of heaven anyway. But I can tell you what the Lord has done in my life of singleness.

I think that there is a special place in the Lord's heart for those who are alone, in the sense of not having a mate. I have sensed His closeness in even tangible ways, especially in the difficult times. When I was going through my time of separation and would sometimes cry myself to sleep, there were times that I felt the physical touch of someone holding me and loving away the hurt and pain. I knew He was always there to listen to me and to let me unburden what I had in my heart. He lifted me out of that place and restored the confidence in knowing that He still had a plan for my life. The devil had tried to steal that confidence from me and make me think that I could not be used, at least not in any significant way. After all, I was a divorced woman! I felt like I had a giant "D" tattooed on me, that stood for *Divorced* or *Damaged*. I'm so glad that God showed me that he is a God of the second chances! Even though mankind sometimes still walks in their manmade rules of judgments and reject people for use in the Kingdom of God, we have a God that looks at the heart and doesn't dispose of us due to life's circumstances.

Married people tell me all the time that it doesn't mean that you can't still feel *alone* at times. Even in the best of marriages there is obviously the need to have intimacy with the Lord and there are places in our lives that He and He alone can fill. But I have always felt that there is a special closeness that is available to tap into with the Lord for the widows, the children in adverse circumstances, for those who are really hurting. It is a place where you feel wrapped in His love and that you know that you are protected. You have the assurance that you are precious in His sight and that He knows your deepest needs and desires.

I don't know whether I will finish my life as a single woman or not. It really isn't my desire to do so, but I have always told the Lord that if I can serve Him better as a single person that I put my *singleness* on His altar and believe Him for the grace to walk that out. If I can work together with a mate and we can bring more glory to Him through that union, then I trust Him to bring the right person to me to have our paths join! Either way I am so thankful to know and to have experienced tremendous intimacy with the Lord through all of my life's experiences.

If you find yourself in a situation similar to this, please know that there is a Heavenly Father who is waiting to embrace you. It isn't just a religious platitude to say that "He is there for you"; it is a reality more real than your next breath. Just cry out to Him from the sincerity of your heart and know that you will find Him and begin to truly know Him in ways that you never imagined!

23

I Will Build My Church

*Matthew 16:18b "...I will build my church, and the gates of
Hades (Hell) will not overcome it."*

Church planting has always been at the forefront of what
Servant Ministries has done. Every outreach, every program or
activity has always been based on showing the love of God to the
people of Guatemala. Every seed of showing God's love is
coupled with believing for those seeds to lead people to
understanding their need to have a personal relationship with the
Lord.

When we first started working in the mountain villages,
there was usually no evangelical Christian church present. The
Mayans had their practices and beliefs which were based in
animism or the worship of creation rather than the Creator.

We would go hut-to-hut and share with the people. In that
time it was rare to find someone who could read and so it was
hard to tell them what the Word of God proclaimed and to allow
them to see it for themselves. There is something inside the

human heart that connects with the truth and recognizes it when it is presented and that is how we began.

Small groups were brought together to begin to teach and to encourage them to make a personal decision to accept the Lord into their lives. Discipleship classes were given to help the people know how to live. We had to start with the basics. I remember one of our first *leaders* being surprised when we told him that he shouldn't beat his wife; a report that had been brought to our attention. In his culture that was totally acceptable; the way to control his wife.

I love reading biographies about missionaries working in remote areas. Two old classics that I will recommend are Peace Child and Lords of the Earth by Don Richardson. It is amazing to see how even amongst cannibalistic tribal people that missionaries found many ancient beliefs within their culture that pointed the way to Christ being the fulfillment for what they had been awaiting. There is only one true God and He is the Creator of the universe. There is something within the human spirit that craves spirituality and looks for fulfillment for it in all kinds of places. But there is only one way to really fill it.

Quoting words of Jesus John 14:6 says *"I am the way, the truth and the life. No one comes to the Father except through me."* God uses people to help transmit the message of the Good News or the Gospel to the world. The good news being that God loves them so much that He paid the price and made it possible for mankind to be brought back into a personal relationship with Him and to know that they have eternal life.

It is one thing to be prepared for eternity which is very important. But it is another thing to be prepared for the earthly life that we still are engaged in. That is what building the church, the true church of Jesus Christ, is all about. It doesn't matter the name of the sign that is over the church door where you attend. If it is a good Bible teaching church, it will show you how to begin your spiritual walk with God, how to grow in your spiritual relationship with God and how to faithfully serve Him. There is no better way to live!

Servant Ministries has been privileged to start a number of churches and we continue to look for new areas to raise up and to let the Word of God bring true transformation to the people's lives.

Church service in Marimba

Worship team in La Puente

Church in Jocotán.

Church in Oquen

Church in El Tular

24

The Pig Story

This is a favorite story that is told to most of the teams who have come down; especially as we are going to enjoy some ham or bacon at our meal! When I went to the mission field, I had only one semester of Spanish at a community college...unless you count a semester in 7th grade! I was not encouraged to go to language school by the people I was working with and so it was just *learning as you go*. After we had been in Guatemala for a year, there was another North American family that came down to work with us and they were going to go to language school in Antigua and we decided to go also. We studied for a full month there, which really helped.

Since I had already picked up a fair bit of Spanish my teacher initially did a lot of talking to me, just to see how much I comprehended. My teacher's name was Alma, and the following was a story that she shared with me.

Alma's mother was a social worker that worked for the government. She was sent out to visit different communities and sometimes that involved staying overnight. On such a visit to a rural mountain village, she found her contact person, a woman that she would be staying with. The woman showed her a very rustic hut where she would be sleeping. Alma's mother asked

"Where is the bathroom?" The woman waved her arm out over the open field and answered "Out there!" Minutes later the hosting woman returned to the hut and handed Alma's mother a stick. Alma's mother asked, "What is the stick for?" The reply came, "That's for when you go to the bathroom....to keep the pigs away!" Now I will interject here and confirm that I continue to hear this from the people even today; that pigs apparently love to eat human feces. It is common for a child that is stooping in the weeds to go to the bathroom to have a pig approach and pretty much suck it right from the child's bottom! Yeah I know, pretty gross!

Alma's mother went back to her office and announced that they definitely needed to do a community latrine in this village. At that time the government had concrete latrines that they would use for such cases and it was set up to take one to this location. Upon installation, Alma's mother called the village people together and explained the need to use the latrine, the health benefits of using it, etc.

Alma's mother went back to the village a month later so that she could see how the project was going. She was surprised to see that the latrine was empty and not being used. She called the village people to a meeting. She asked if there was a problem and encouraged them to tell her if there was. The people were silent. She shared that she would do whatever she could to solve any issues but that she first had to be made aware of them. The Mayan people are very reserved, especially with people that they do not know. One man finally raised his hand and said "It is cold to sit on!" As this was in the highlands that was understandable and plans were made to put an animal hide or piece of fabric on the cement seat to avoid the *coldness*. Alma's mother continued to ask if there were any other problems. It took a lot of prodding and patience but finally one other man raised his hand and said "If we use that, what are the pigs going to eat?" True story! I then explain to the teams that I buy imported pork!

25

Midwife Impromptu

In the United States there is a stereotype that every pastor's wife should be able to play the piano and maybe teach Sunday School. It is a little different in Guatemala! Many times the pastor's wife, especially in times past, is called upon to help with a birthing. Back when I was living in Jocotán, in the earlier years, Hortencia (Pastor Armando's wife) showed up at my door one evening. She asked me if I had any thread. Assuming that she needed to sew a button on or some such thing, I got her a spool of sewing thread. She then told me that she had a woman that had just given birth and that she was hemorrhaging a lot. She needed to sew her up and wanted something heavier. The only thing that I could find in my house was some cinnamon flavored dental floss. Hortencia left with that and came back the next day to tell me that it had worked just fine!!!

26

Let Your Fingers Do The Walking?

...I Don't Think So!

This happened back in the mid-90s. I was helping some other missionaries to make the trip by land to Belize....as I had done the trip through Mexico many times. A teenager, Maleia also accompanied us and she and I took a boat across to Guatemala for a visit while the others stayed in Belize.

Maleia and I were making a trip down the mountain to Chiquimula. I had an appointment to call one of the pastors from my church. At that time there were no phones in town. The closest available phones were an hour bus ride away and then you had to go to the local phone company and wait until they could get an international call to go through. Maleia and I got on the local *chicken bus* and started down the mountain. I was sitting right behind the driver on the aisle seat and Maleia was behind me. A short ways into our ride, I was startled as a flame of fire shot out of the motor cover, right at my feet. Sorry, but the automatic reaction was a scream....which sent the bus into a panic! While the bus was coming to a stop, people had kicked out two windows and opened the back emergency door and were jumping out. We all vacated the bus and five minutes later they told us all to get back on. Now, we hadn't seen a tool box or any assurance that the problem was taken care of, but we got back on. Seeing the driver's helper with a five gallon bucket of water as he stood next to the driver didn't give us a lot of confidence either. This time both of us were seated behind the driver and less than a half mile down the road, we had a repeat of another flame shooting out. The bus stopped again and Maleia begged me, "Nancy, please don't make me get back on that bus!" Others on the bus shared her feelings. I explained that we would be stranded, halfway down the mountain, if we didn't get back on...but that was the decision we made! Half of the bus waited alongside the road, at the mercy of waiting for someone that would pick them up. We finally found a pickup that managed to cram us in, with us straddling the tailgate and getting a real dust bath as we continued down the dirt road. We finally made it to the phone company and of course the international lines were down. By the time I got my call placed, we were 2-3 hours late and the pastor's first comment was "I was expecting your call earlier!" Well with going through two bus fires, being stranded, having a ride from a stranger and still having to walk to get to the phone company.....it was definitely not "Let your fingers do the walking through the yellow pages!" Welcome to third world living!

27

Pioneer Dentistry

In 1990 we had a dental hygienist come to visit us. Bev had been encouraged by the dentist she worked with to come down and be prepared to do what she could do to help people. Back in those days, she didn't think that she could transport any meds and so came with her tools but no anesthesia. We went up to one of our high mountain villages, La Puente, where both the pastor and his wife had great need of some dental work being done.

Pastor Emilio, being the gentleman that he is, decided to let his wife go first! Rosalia sat on a rock; that was her dental chair. Her teeth were broken off at the gums with decayed pieces sticking out and there were major problems in most of her teeth, or what was left of them. Bev began to work on her, without any ability to numb her up. I stood in front of her and told her to take my hands and to squeeze when she had pain. I thought she would break my fingers but she never cried out. It was a very long process, that involved digging up into the gums and bone but the job was completed.

Pastor Emilio, after witnessing what his wife had gone through, opted to wait on his dental work! Can't say as I blame him! About three weeks later Rosalia came down the mountain specifically to look for us as she normally did not come into town. She wanted to thank us! She said that her mouth was healing up fine and that it was the first time in many years that she didn't have any pain in her mouth. As difficult as her experience had been, she was thankful and grateful and wanted to express that to us! How many of us get concerned with a minor toothache and can't get into a dentist quick enough? How many things do we take for granted, that the assistance or help that we need will be readily available? Can we even imagine what it is like for someone to have years of chronic mouth pain and the suffering that is involved? I'm glad that we could help Rosalia but even more glad that we can now offer much more modern and comfortable dental assistance! In the following years, we were able to help provide both Pastor Emilio and Rosalia with full dentures!

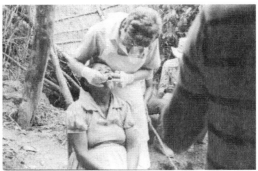

Rosalia receiving her dental care.

28

Sacrifices to Be Made, Joys to Be Shared

Matthew 16:24 " Then Jesus said to his disciples, if anyone would come after me, he must deny himself and take up his cross and follow me."

I believe that we have within our grasp the ability to really fulfill all that God has designed for us, but that comes with a cost. I would rather dream big and reach 75% of what I have dreamed and believed God to bring to fulfillment than to have dreamed only small dreams or never to have dreamed at all.

I had a dream once about a huge warehouse in heaven. The Lord was showing me, with heaviness in His heart, all of the "unclaimed provisions and dreams" that still were being stored there. His children had not procured them due to a lack of passion or diligence in their lives; to lives that were being lived so far below what He had destined for them.

John 10:10 tells us that "The thief comes only to steal and kill and destroy; but I (Jesus) have come that they may have life and have it to the full." I believe that with all of my heart. I think that we all live below what God really desires for us. Some things are easy to detect as the devil's attempt to kill, steal and destroy; sickness, accidents, dissension with people and a multitude of other things; but what about the more subtle things? What about a measure of compromise because others are doing it, what about complacency, mediocrity, or settling for what we know is not our best? *Luke 12:48 "...from everyone who has been given much; much will be demanded..."* I believe that the more we tap into God's full purpose for our lives, the more we will experience, but it does come with a cost! I have always told people coming to the mission field that "Your highs will be higher and your lows will be lower." I believe this is true for anyone who is truly sold out to the Lord's purposes for your life. The enemy doesn't care if you are faithful to church attendance, if you do occasional praying or try to be what the world views as a good person. Oh, but if you try to really fulfill what God has for you in its fullness, now there is someone that draws the enemy's attention and he will try to dissuade.

There are movies that I don't feel comfortable watching that other Christians can watch. There are books that I choose not to read or conversations that I remove myself from or shows on the television that I have to turn off, because my heart's desire is to see the fullness of what He has shown me in my heart that my life can possess. Mediocrity or a life that is *better than most* doesn't require that much of us. But I know what the Lord has put into my heart and I want to see His greatness be made manifest in this earthly realm and not wait to experience it until I am in heaven. To some I know that I will be viewed as a fanatic, as being too zealous, but I have had a glimpse of what is possible. I know that I will not reach perfection in this life. I know that I fall short and that I sometimes do what I do not want to do, falling back into what is easy for my flesh to act out. But my heart wants to pay the price and I ask the Lord on a regular basis to help me to fulfill all that He has for me and to allow me to be used of Him.   I want to see His glory be made manifest in my earthly life; that I can share it with others. A sacrifice isn't really a sacrifice in comparison to the potential joy that can come from a completely sold out life lived for the Lord!

29

My Spiritual Journey

I was raised in a traditional church. I was taught good morals, the difference from right and wrong, the fear of God and had a lot of Bible knowledge. I'm thankful for that foundation. I did not understand that I had to have a personal relationship with God or that it was even possible. I basically thought that I was to live by the Golden Rule and be a good person and that would get me to heaven. Now while it is wonderful to be a good person, I have learned that no one can be *good enough* to earn salvation or eternal life. We all blow it, we all mess up and we all have a need for a personal Savior.

I married my first boyfriend, after a four year long-distance courtship and got married the same month that I graduated from high school in 1970. We had our first child three years later, something that I was really ready for. I had always wanted to be a wife and a mom. Hank was born March 20, 1973. Three years later our daughter, Julie, was born on March 23, 1976. By this time my husband had begun to drink heavily and was an alcoholic. Life became increasingly hard as I never knew if my husband would be home at night or not. If I wanted to spend time with him it meant doing the party scene, which was not my thing! I was going to church, but again not understanding what it was really about. I would be out on

Saturday night until the bars closed and then in the church choir on Sunday morning and teaching Sunday School. My heart was not at peace. I told my husband that this was not the life that I wanted for our children; that they deserved better. He agreed that both the children and I deserved better and his solution was to leave. I had hoped that he would change! He did leave and left me with two small children to raise alone.

Thank God that I at least knew where to turn, to recognize that God could help me! I didn't know the Roman's Road (scriptures pertaining to salvation) or what a born-again Christian was, but I cried out to the Lord from the depths of my heart. It was a Sunday in the summer of 1978. I had just left church. I remember talking to a neighbor on the way out of the parking lot, sitting in my car. Tears streamed down my face and I had a pounding headache in the temples of my head that had been with me for basically nine months. I had reached my breaking point! I got home and got the kids in the house, who were two and five years old at the time. I went to my bedroom and fell upon my bed sobbing; I could not hold it in any longer. I cried out to God and acknowledged that I could not do this on my own and asked Him to help me. I know that this was my point of conversion or of surrendering my life to the Lord. I didn't even know the scripture *Romans 10:9-10* at that point, but I know that God met me in that moment of my life.

The Lord began to do a work in me. He brought a born-again Christian across my path and I began to understand what had taken place in my life. I used to read the Bible and attended a Bible study but now it had more understanding for me. Life was still hard but I had a place to turn for strength. The separation in my marriage lasted for eight years before my husband divorced me and remarried. He had become a born again spirit-filled Christian for which I am very grateful! He was also very good to take care of our needs economically! I had believed for the restoration of my marriage but that did not come about. I have learned that I will never understand some things this side of heaven and that is okay. I can leave those things in God's hands. God has given each of us the freedom of choice and a free will which we have the right to exercise.

Even though my marriage was not restored, God was doing some amazing things in my life and causing me to grow spiritually. I can look back now and see the steps that He took to prepare me for what He knew would be my future. But I have not forgotten my day to day life, while I was raising my children. God was there for me and helped me every step of the way.

I learned to stop trying to figure out everything that happened in my life. Every day we have a choice as to how we are going to live. I started attending a good Bible teaching spirit-filled church where I really grew in my spiritual walk. I became involved in the children's ministry in the church and shortly thereafter began to work as a receptionist at the church.

My relationship with the Lord is what has given me the strength to move forward and to do what I have done. I believe that any person with a hungry heart, who is trying to answer questions, who is looking for understanding of life itself, will find their answers in God. He knows exactly where you are at, what you are feeling, and that He and He alone can fill that empty place in your heart. We all have that place in us; it is how He created us. He is the only one that can fill it.

Your past doesn't matter, where you have been or what you have done. It doesn't matter if you were raised in the church or have any knowledge of what the Bible says. I just want to encourage you to know where to look. When you realize that life isn't what you thought it would be, when things are falling apart and you feel alone and scared, when life just doesn't make sense; God is there waiting for you! Give Him a chance to enter into your life, to take the helm of your life and to direct your decisions! He will do amazing things and you will know what it is to have true peace and joy; peace and joy that are not affected by the changing circumstances of life! There is a constant and continuous knowing that no matter what is happening in your life, that there is Someone who is there with you to carry you every step of the way!

30

It can Change your Life

I know the power of participating in a mission trip! My life was forever changed when I went on one. I had no idea how those 10 days would revolutionize my life! For me, it was my first face-to-face with true poverty. It stirred something in my heart. It gave me compassion to reach out to those in need. It changed my value system.

Long after I got home, the emotions stayed with me. For me, it turned into making a commitment to actually go to the mission field to live and work long term. My life has never been the same and I'm so glad for that.

Going on that short term outreach made me look at things differently after I went home. It made me think about what was really important. It made some of my materialistic desires seem so petty compared to the daily needs and hand to mouth existence that I had witnessed. It made me thankful for all that I had.

I wish more churches would get the heart to do mission teams. It doesn't take away from your local church, it adds so much more. People come home with a new passion, with a spark and they are looking for a way and place to use it. Local churches receive the blessing and fruit of what takes place in a participant's heart; that has been touched by this experience and now looks for a way to express it. I truly commend the churches, who not only write out monthly checks to support missions but also get the hands-on involvement to go for themselves. They have the opportunity to know the missionaries that they support, to know their hearts, their needs, their passion, their dreams. And they can connect and become a part of that! You leave something behind of yourself every time to you go on a mission trip. The local people where you visited hold that part and they long for your return or for others like you. A connection has been made, in such a short time frame, but it is real and longs to stay alive by you fanning its flame!

I know people feel intimidated by not knowing the language, by not feeling qualified or having anything to offer. Language doesn't have to be a barrier; just reach out and be friendly and show love through your interaction with the people and through your labor. Your presence, your willingness to work side by side with the nationals, to be involved, speaks volumes to the people. Just come with a serving heart and you will be amazed at what can happen. Most of the time the participants feel that they are taking back home so much more than they gave. It is true that it is a two way experience and everyone benefits by what transpires.

Everyone should try it! Some may only go once, but they go home impacted and may choose to support a ministry on the field through their prayers and financial support. But their prayers are more heartfelt and their offering generally more consistent due to what they experienced. Others, once they have gotten a taste for it, come back again and again! Some connect with one area and continue to come back and build relationships with the nationals and become a part of their lives. Others go to a variety of places and are stirred by what they experience from place to place. Others may see themselves doing something longer term or something that they could do after retirement. Whatever the case may be for you, take the step to experience visiting another culture and become a part in what is happening there! Reach out and make a difference in the lives of others! You will see your life changed too!

Team from Michigan.

Team in Camotán's Church.

Visiting churches.

Construction team.

Medical team.

31

Benedicto… First Name Basis with the Village Witch

We were working with a Bible Institute from the capital called C.E.M.I. It was a one year live-in Bible School course that gave an emphasis to missions. It was founded and overseen by some North Americans. I can't even remember how we crossed paths but it was one of those divine connections from God. They had excellent teaching resources but were looking for some *hands-on practical experience* for their students. We had that to offer. They began to send us two students every weekend. I would take them up to La Puente, one of the first churches that we planted back in 1990 that is waaaay up in the mountains. We gave them a variety of ways to get involved and do outreaches. At the end of their year, the school made it a requirement for all of the students (17 of them) to come to Jocotán and stay with us for seven weeks. They wanted us to take them to an untouched area up in the mountains, one that had never been evangelized. They had seven weeks to plant a church there. They had to live like the people did, hunt their fire wood, grind their corn by hand to make their tortillas, cook their own food; all while they went hut to hut every day evangelizing and had a church service every night. We divided the groups into two teams. One spent a week in the mountain village while the other team spent that time in town, which gave them a little bit of a break and still kept them busy and involved.

The village was Tunucó Abajo and it is known as a center for witchcraft in our area. People come from other areas to be trained in the practices of witchcraft. Benedicto was the head witch of the seven witches that the village had. He came to me and put his finger in my face and said "Until you came I could keep the Christians out of here. I am praying curses on you!" I silently praised God that we (the Christians) had been able to penetrate this village and thanked Him also for His protection over us. A church was raised up in that seven weeks. I can't remember the exact number but a number of people had accepted the Lord and were water baptized. It was the beginning of a church in this village. I am still in contact with a number of these students after all of these years. Ana, our clinic nurse, was one of those students.

Here are a couple more incidents involving the village of Tunucó.

Adela was the first Guatemalan friend that I had made when I began in Guatemala. She would help me with my Spanish and help me translate some children's material into Spanish to use for a Sunday School class. We were having a three day evangelistic crusade in the village of Tunucó. Adela worked in this village with a school. She planned to come down the mountain after she finished work and then go back up the mountain with us to attend our meetings. Just before we were to leave, we received word that she had been in an accident. She was getting a ride down the mountain in a large truck and the brakes gave out. Her leg was almost completely severed and she died shortly afterwards. The atmosphere in the village when we arrived was so heavy, so dark, so oppressing! Amongst our grief we had our service but it was dead, there was no life to it and it went beyond just our grief. I attended Adela's funeral the next day as they have to bury within 24 hours since they don't embalm people. Right after the burial, we left for our second day of services in Tunucó. I was still grieving the loss of my friend but the atmosphere had totally changed in the village. The heaviness was gone. We had a wonderful service and people gave their lives to the Lord. The demonic presence had been broken and we saw a breakthrough. Was Adela's *accident* just that, an accident? Adela had stood up to Benedicto and defended what we were doing! I know that vehicles have mechanical breakdowns and defects but I also know what we *felt* in that village on the day that Adela died. Something was going on in the spiritual realm, something very dark and ugly.

Here is another incident that happened in Tunucó:

It was getting close to Christmas in 1997. We had just gone up to the church in Tunucó to hold a special Christmas service and hand out toy bags to the kids. The church was not right off the road and you had to walk down the mountain to where our vehicle was parked. Pastor Armando (pastor from Jocotán), Jason and Theresa (North American workers that were with me at that time) accompanied me on this trip. On the way walking down the mountain from the church I fell and hurt myself quite seriously. It took a number of men to carry me down to the vehicle. Back then Pastor Armando didn't know how to drive. Jason had never driven in the mountains but it was up to him to get us down the mountain. We were pretty sure that my leg was broken from the way that it was hanging and I was in extreme pain. It was a long trip down the mountain as they stopped a number of times when I got to the point of passing out from the pain. The town doctor took one look at me in the vehicle and told them to take me to the hospital in Chiquimula.

He gave me two shots that were supposed to help with the pain, but I don't know how much they helped. I had crushed my right ankle and broken the leg. It was the ankle that was the real problem! They said it came very close to severing an artery and that, if it had, I would never have made it to medical help in time. They told me that I would need surgery and that I still may never walk right again. They put me in a cast and we waited a week until after Christmas when they put a plate and five pins in my ankle. I was in a cast for three months and couldn't put any weight on it for over four months. I had over a year of physical therapy and they finally said that no more could be done, even though I was still lacking 15 degrees of my flex in the ankle which obviously affects my walking on uneven ground. Was this experience too an *accident*? Or was it the prayers and curses of a village witch trying to get my influence out of that village and to take me out? I had a lot of time to reflect on that in my recovery period. My conclusion was this! What the enemy meant for harm against me, I was asking the Lord to bring me back twice as committed to the work that I was doing. My prayer was that the enemy would regret having brought this attack against me because it was going to backfire! I believe that the Lord honored my request and I believe that I have had a deeper passion for what I am doing as a result of this incident! As Joyce Meyer's says, "A difficult situation will make you *more bitter* or *more better*! I chose to come out *better*!

32

I Think I Have a Problem

It was June of 1991. I had just taken two Bible School students home that lived a few hours the other side of the capital. I had an airline ticket to fly back to the United States the following day for my son's graduation from high school. I was heading down a dirt winding road that would lead out to the main highway. I could see down the road around the curve that a small car was barreling down the road very fast and very much out of control. I decided to pull over on the edge of the road and to give them lots of space to get by me. They didn't get by me but crashed right into me. They bounced off me and then hit the mountain on the other side of the road and came to a stop. I was stunned. I had been spun around and my back tires were hanging off the side of the mountain and my front tires were in the air and I was teetering on the side of the mountain. I didn't realize this until I climbed down from my vehicle. Three men got out of the other vehicle and staggered toward me, all of them very drunk. One was waving a checkbook assuring me that they would settle up with me and I knew that likely the check wasn't worth the paper it was written on. I didn't know what to do.

Someone asked me if I wanted them to call the police and I said yes, still thinking like a North American since I had only been in Guatemala a couple of years. Most accidents were settled between drivers without involving the law. In the meantime a truck stopped and asked if I wanted them to pull my jeep back onto the road. There were houses below in the ravine and the jeep could have easily fallen down there. They pulled it to the road and there were some awful noises and it left something lying on the side of the road, that I later learned was my transmission. There was a strong smell of gasoline because they had ruptured the gas tank.

The police showed up and piled us all into their vehicle. I didn't think too much of it since I knew that I couldn't drive my vehicle and figured that there was some sort of paperwork to fill out. Once back at the police station, the realization came upon me that I had a problem when they began to fingerprint me!

It was raining and I was cold, wet and in need of a bathroom. I asked the police if I could use one. I was ignored! I waited a little more and my need became more urgent. I asked again and was informed that there was no bathroom. I inquired how a jail with prisoners and their staff could not have facilities. He told me that there was one but it didn't work very well and that I couldn't use it. I looked him in the face and asked him if I could go outdoors. I was sent out with two policemen that had their guns pulled and aimed at me. We walked three blocks through town and I was told "here", indicating that I could do what I had to do, right in front of houses. Thank God back in those days I always wore a skirt or it could have been worse. They never so much as turned their backs. We returned to the police station.

I learned that no paperwork could be filled out since one of the men had been taken to the hospital and we would have to wait for him to be released. Another one of the men that had been in the accident knew just enough English to be aggravating.

He tried to convince me to say that the accident had been my fault. Knowing that I was a missionary he reasoned that God would provide me with another car or the funds to fix this one. When I didn't consent to that he became abusive and started using some very inappropriate language with me. My car had been towed into town and was around the corner from the police station. I asked if I could go wait in my car. They consented but again sent me with the two armed policemen, with their guns pulled, that escorted me to the jeep. I was told to be back in the police station by 5:00am. I got a little sleep and at least was a little warmer and managed to find my own bathroom, without the eyes of the policemen watching me. There was a knock on the window and it was the man that had been released from the hospital, with a cup of coffee in his hand that he was offering me. Once he sobered up, he felt very bad and told me that he was a back-slidden Christian. He believed that I was an angel, sent by God; that had saved their lives. He understood well that if they had not hit my vehicle that they would have gone off the mountainside and it could have been much worse. He promised me to get back into church.

I found out that the law in Guatemala, at that time, made all drivers be put under arrest. You were guilty until things were sorted out and your innocence proven. You are also responsible to find your own legal counsel. The three decided who the driver had been, although it was not the one who really had been driving. He and I were detained. The other two were free to go find legal counsel for their friend. I was on my own and couldn't leave. In all the movies I have seen, a prisoner always has the right to make a phone call so I asked to make mine. I found out that there were no phones at the police station, but again I was taken at gunpoint with my guards and walked through town to the public phone company where I was allowed to make my call.

A North American ran up to me to find out what was going on. He worked for the local cable company and after my brief explanation he told me that he knew the judge and would inform him. I called a missionary friend in the capital who said that he would come help me.

News travels fast and more so when it involves a foreigner. A local lawyer came by the police station and convinced the police that as a North American that I had a right to use their bathroom facilities. From that time on, they did let me use their bathroom but still brought me no food. My friend, Van, arrived and left with the other two men that were helping the *driver* who was being held. They later came back with a document. It was very vague and stated that it was dusk when the accident happened and hard to see well, etc. It said that one of the *passengers* of the other car was offering to pay for the repairs to my vehicle, who in fact really had been the driver. I told Van that it neglected some basic details, like the fact that all three were highly inebriated. Van told me that they were scared that this would hurt them in finding employment or marking their record and reminded me that I was getting what I needed, my car fixed. I consented and signed the document. I was released into Van's custody and didn't have to spend the second night at the police station. I was never put into the cell since this was a men's jail and they had been discussing the need to send me to a women's jail. Van is a real evangelist and had taken advantage of the situation to witness to the prisoners and led 13 of them to salvation!

I was able to go home with Van and take a shower and get some food and sleep before reporting back the next morning when we had an appointment with the judge. The judge met with me first. He pointed out that the documents were pretty vague and that he wasn't sure whose fault it was and asked me if I felt it had been mine. I told him in no uncertain terms that I had not been at fault. He asked me if there was something else that I wanted to add to the account. Trying to protect their reputations I added that they had been driving faster than they should have and were not being very prudent in their driving. I'm sure the judge got the idea.

When it was all said and done, I was released officially after being under arrest for 49 hours. The men left with their bank accounts emptied. My friends found out that American Airlines would honor my airline ticket that had been for two days prior, with proof that I had been in jail, and allow me on the next day's flight. Just in case you need to know that!

A local mechanic had somewhat reconnected my transmission but it would only drive 10-15 miles an hour and I still did not have a gas tank. Guatemalans can be very resourceful so they put five gallon open buckets of gasoline in my back seat and had a hose running from my motor to draw it out of the buckets. One of the men involved in the accident insisted on riding with me so that he could change the hose from bucket to bucket. It took us all night to get back to the capital. We took my jeep to a relative of one of the men that had a car repair shop.

I had a couple of issues to resolve before going to the airport. Back in those days, your vehicle was stamped into your passport. You could not leave the country without your vehicle or you had to leave your vehicle in possession of the government, assuring your return and not the sale of your vehicle in the country. We went to the appropriate office. They sent a worker to go see the jeep at the repair shop. Part way there, he told me that he would sign the papers and allow me to leave without seeing the vehicle because he knew that I would not make it to the airport in time for my flight. The other issue was that I had a paper stating that I was no longer a prisoner of the state of Guatemala that I was to present to the main office of immigration, thereby allowing me permission to leave the country. Again there was no time to do that and I reasoned that I could give it to the immigration officials at the airport.

The plane was loading by the time I got to the airport. I was told the gate number and I took off running. I got my passport stamped and all of the normal steps and then handed them the paper as I was leaving saying that it needed to go to the immigration office. I got down to the second gate when the policemen came running after me, telling me that I could not leave and that I had to come back with them to the office.

I really was at about the end of my rope at this point. I really wanted to leave Guatemala! When the head official presented himself at the doorway of his office; it all came spilling out and I could have won an academy award. There was no time for the normal expected cordial greetings; I just let him have it with both barrels. I told him that I didn't know why I was being treated this way. I had come to Guatemala to help their people. I told him that I hadn't been fed by the police and that they had made me urinate on the street. I told them that my son was going to graduate from high school; that I was his mother and he was my only son and that I had to be there for him. I asked him in no uncertain terms what I had to do to get on that plane. All of this was done with a whole lot of emotion and very quickly, knowing that the plane was loading. The man reached out and patted my shoulder and told me to calm down and that he would let me on the plane after he was assured that I planned to come back. He went on to explain that he could not receive the document that I had tried to leave with them and that it would in fact have to go to the central office for immigration. He informed me that when I got back to Guatemala that the very first thing that I had to do immediately was to go to the immigration office and explain why this hadn't been settled before I left the country. He told me that upon entering the plane that I would be considered a fugitive of Guatemala. I told him that I didn't care and got on the plane.

I made it back in time for my son's graduation. I returned to Guatemala and got more than a few chuckles at the immigration office as they listened to my account, although they did in fact have me listed as a fugitive. I was picked up on a motorcycle by one of the men from the accident and taken to pick up my repaired vehicle. So I must say that my missionary resume is a bit tarnished as it includes some jail time and being a fugitive!

33

Divine Appointment in a Hot Tub

I am convinced that God has a sense of humor. He is the creator of all of the emotions that He has given us and I have seen this side of His nature. The following is such an occasion.

I was attending a Rodney Howard-Browne Camp Meeting in Louisville, KY in 1993. I was with a couple of women from my church as well as some youth that were with us. I announced to the rest of my roommates that I was going to go down and use the hot tub for a bit before we left for the evening service. When I got to the hot tub there were two men already there; one elderly and one about my age. We were all there to attend the conference and began to talk and share with one another. When I shared that I had been doing mission work in Guatemala, Larry (the one my age), spoke up and told me that he had a daughter who felt she was called to missions and felt called to the country of Guatemala. Nita was the same age as my son. We exchanged contact information during the conference and I later gave Nita a call and asked her if she wanted to accompany me on a road trip from Michigan to Guatemala. I stopped and picked her up on my way through Texas, never having met her in person. That was the beginning of a long term relationship in which Nita came down to Guatemala on multiple occasions and a friendship with both her and her parents that has lasted for 20 years now.

Larry has a couple of used car lots and has blessed me on many occasions to have the use of a vehicle while I am doing my fundraising trips in the United States. He introduced me to my first time usage of a cell phone; I thought I had died and gone to heaven! The family has been good friends and supporters of the ministry to this day. It all began in a hot tub! God has his divine connections and appointments that He puts in our paths; they just sometime happen in a way that we are not expecting.

34

Adopt-a-Child Activity

Adopt-a-Child is an activity that began back in the 1990s with our in-coming teams and has stood the test of time and become one of the favorites and impacting experiences for those who participate in it. The idea is to give both the team member and the Guatemalan child that is chosen to be a part of this outreach the opportunity to have a unique experience to know one another. We have seen how in the midst of language barriers, different cultures and vast differences in lifestyles that the love of God still finds a means to be expressed and shown.

In the beginning we would choose children from the mountain churches or our pastors' children and match them up one on one with the members of in-coming teams that come to visit. We would load them up in a privately rented bus which right off the bat was a first time experience for many of the children. We went to Chiquimula to a Pollo Campero (Guatemalan's version of a KFC) for an early lunch. I figured chicken was an easy choice as you are allowed to eat with your fingers and not be concerned too much about table manners. We still had to fish the occasional bone off the floor under the table or stop the child from eating the bone; having meat to eat was not the norm for these children. The team members were instructed to take their child into the bathroom and accomplish the necessary bathroom needs, not an easy feat for children who had never seen a toilet before.

I will never forget one Canadian pastor coming out and telling of his experience in the bathroom. He took his boy into the bathroom and pointed at the toilet. Mario was a smart kid and picked it up quickly and proceeded to point to the toilet. Pastor Paul then tried sitting down on the toilet, hoping to get the point across. Mario mimicked the action perfectly, dunking his long shirt tail into the toilet bowl and getting it very wet. Pastor Paul finally conceded that there was only one way to get the job done and had to give the practical version of Toilet Use 101 and it worked like a charm!

Another team member came out of his bathroom mission, without his child and told us that he couldn't get the child to leave. The child was fascinated with the sink faucet and the automatic hand dryer and kept repeatedly washing his hands, drying them and then going back to washing again so that he could again use the dryer. We had to convince him that his hands were clean enough.

After having lunch we would take the children to the local outdoor market and buy them shoes and clothing; dressing them from head to foot. Sometimes team members threw in more of their own money and the kids were set up with soccer balls, dolls, and a variety of other items. The kids' eyes were wide with amazement as they were allowed to pick out things that they liked.

After the shopping excursion we loaded up in the bus again and took the kids to a local public pool where we played with them. All of the initial apprehensions, on both sides, had been melted. No longer were there fears of how to communicate, how to interact etc. Something happened and a bond had been formed, in the midst of all odds. Now it was just a group of adults having fun with a bunch of kids. You could see the transformation in the children as well. You can only imagine what their apprehensions had been initially, being left by their parents and being told that they were to stay with this unknown adult for the day. Guatemalan children, especially those in the mountains, are robbed of their childhood as North Americans know it. They are taught at a very young age how to go out and hunt for firewood, to carry water and to be responsible for younger siblings. They don't know what it is to be allowed the chance to just play and have fun for a day and it is an amazing thing to watch them enjoy.

After our swim, the kids were nice and clean and all of their new clothes and shoes were put on. Hair was fixed and photos were taken of the child with their "mom or dad for the day" as a remembrance for them to take home. We then drove home where their parents were waiting to receive them.

Once our Embrace program (child sponsorship program) began in 2000, we would use our children that did not have a sponsor and were on our waiting list, awaiting one. We told both the child's family and the team members that there was no commitment on either side. It was the opportunity to spend a special day with a special child and show them the love of God. But many times, the team member made the decision to become the child's sponsor. After all, they had met the children and spent time with them. It had become personal and a wonderful opportunity to reach out and make a lasting difference to these children and their family. The child would begin to receive the benefits that an Embrace sponsor provides, benefits that make a long term difference.

After it was all over, it was wonderful to hear of the team members' comments. Many expressed their apprehension in how it would be, being placed with a child that they could not understand or communicate with, etc. But it was also awesome to hear how those barriers had all disappeared when they just made the decision to make the day be about the children and showing them love! One testimony I will never forget:

Bob was from Michigan and had come down on a construction team and that had been the main focus of their time in Guatemala. Bob had gone to the team leader and told him that he preferred to work on the construction project and not participate in the Adopt-a-Child activity. He was told that it was not optional and that everyone would participate. That night at dinner, after we had had our day with the kids, Bob came to talk to me. He told me that he needed to ask for my forgiveness. I asked him what he needed forgiveness for. He told me that he had been thinking some really negative things against me. I kind of laughed and asked him to explain. He told me that in his mind he was thinking "Who does this woman (me) think she is telling me that I have to potty train a child, etc." He then looked at me with very serious eyes and said "Nancy, I want to thank you; that was the best day of my life!" Bob sponsored his child for many years through the Embrace program. God had touched his heart and given him a very special experience even though he didn't think he even wanted it.

This is the way that we find many of our new Embrace sponsors and it gives both the sponsor and child a very special connection that results in return visits and more days of spending the Adopt-a-Child day together. It also sometimes means home visits to see how the family lives and an on-going relationship that goes so much further than just sending in a monthly check for sponsorship.

Over the years we have changed some of the details of how we operate this Adopt-a-Child activity but it always includes the time together and opportunity to form a very special bond with a very special child.

At the hot baths.

At the pool in the Ministry Center.

Ice breaking time.

Playing with the kids.

One on One time.

35

Famous For All the Wrong Reasons

In the early 90s there was an outbreak of cholera in Jocotán. It had begun in South America and the news gave the calculations as to when they believed it would reach Central America and more specifically Guatemala. It did arrive! It was a terrible thing! Cholera basically claims the lives of the weak and young from dehydration. The symptoms include both extreme vomiting and diarrhea and the person loses their body fluids rapidly. The only treatment was to try to put fluids into the body faster than they were lost. We helped the local health department to build some rustic wooden chairs. There was a hole in the seat where a bucket was placed underneath. There were arms built on the chair to put IVs into both arms. There was another bucket placed in a holder in front of the patient to catch their vomit. Usually by the time the people were brought for help, it was too late and the dehydration claimed their lives. Cholera is highly contagious! The health department went up into the mountain communities to teach the people how to dispose of a body that had succumbed to the disease. They were to be wrapped in plastic to make sure that no body excrements were left on the trails that could infect others. Big campaigns were given to teach the people about better hygiene practices; the need to wash hands before preparing food, after the use of a bathroom, etc. That was one good thing that came out of all of this that still helps the level of hygienic living that we have today; to see fruit and other food that is wrapped in plastic instead of being left out to the flies.

The disease took its toll and claimed the lives of many in Jocotán. Jocotán was named as the *cholera capital of Latin America*! Not just Guatemala, not just Central America but of all of Latin America! It is not the fame that you want for your city!

36

The Trip from Hell

I have made the trip by land from Michigan to Guatemala many times, especially in the earlier years, 13 times to be exact. Our first trip was made with a horse trailer behind us. I came down twice in a school bus and the rest of the times in a variety of vehicles, sometimes to import a vehicle from the United States to use in Guatemala. My most memorable trip was one that took place in 1997. It was the most memorable and the one to convince me to never do another road trip. After reading this you will understand why.

I started the trip from Port Huron, Michigan. I had a young man, Jason, with me. He was coming down to live and to start some projects with the people. His family had given him a pop up tent camper that they had used for family camping to bring along, that was to serve as his *home* upon arrival. Now pop up tent campers have very small tires. I expressed my concern for such a long trip and one that did not include all American expressways but I was assured that it would be fine. We were not even out of visual sight of the driveway when a tire went rolling by on the shoulder of the road. I said to Jason, "I think that belongs to us!" It did in fact belong to the pop up tent camper. Not a good start to what was going to be a very long trip! We got our tire fixed and got back on the road.

En route we hooked up with Theresa, another person that was to make the trip with us. She was also coming down to work with the ministry. She had been down on a short term mission trip with Southeastern Bible College from Lakeland, Florida and decided to make a longer term commitment. The three of us continued on to Texas where we picked up our last trip participant and also another vehicle. Nita had been down to Guatemala with me a number of times and I knew that she was a good driver and up for the challenge. Her dad was donating a car that we were to bring down for Pastor Armando, which was to be his first ever car. I got the privilege of teaching him to drive....but that is another story! The idea was that we would have two vehicles and a relief driver for each one. However, Nita and I wound up doing most of the driving!

We got to the Mexican border and they wanted to see what was inside the camper. Lo and behold the tool that allowed you to open it had been left behind in Texas and it could not be opened. It took a lot of talking and convincing but they finally let us through without inspecting the camper. Now even though I had been assured that the camper would be fine, they had sent along 4-5 spares......not enough! We had blowout after blowout and a flat or two on the car as well. The axle on the camper began to bend and we spent an afternoon and into the night at a shop while they welded some extra support to the axle, hoping it would get us through. The car didn't have air conditioning and it was very hot traveling through Mexico. Those that rode in that vehicle did a lot of sweating. Early in the morning Jason fell asleep at the wheel and went off the road through brush and weeds and banged up the camper pretty good and shaved off all of the reflectors. Now this was more serious! We had blown the last of our tires! There were no more spares and nothing in Mexico that would work on it. It's good that outside of the

United States that they know how to get more creative in how to fix things. They came up with the idea of cutting off some car springs from an old car that had 14" tires on it. They jacked up the camper and put them on it, so that we could use normal size tires on it! The camper looked like it was doing a nose dive but it got us back on the road. Jason was delegated to keep Nita awake as she did the rest of the driving for that vehicle.

We got across the Guatemala border without too much hassle and then we still had to drive about 8-9 hours across the country to reach Jocotán. We were in the home stretch! I was following the camper and could see that the axle that we had repaired was giving out. It was bending more and more. We stopped and talked about it but we were all exhausted, it had been 10 days of hard travel. Nita was determined to get us there, even if she had to drag the camper. We made a little more progress but then the axle almost bent into a full U. There was no further option, we couldn't move forward. I left the camper and other vehicle there on the road and drove the last 30 minutes to Jocotán where I found Pastor Armando, a flatbed truck and a whole bunch of men to come help. They basically had to lift that camper and put it on the trailer which was no easy feat since it was loaded down with stuff and very heavy. That was the last trip that that camper was ever going to make. We did get it to Jocotán and Jason did live in it for several months. We had had 14 blowouts plus all the trouble with the axle twice. I told Nita, "If I ever talk about driving to Guatemala again, please remind me of this trip!" That was in fact my last trip by land! Planes are so much easier!

37

Give me another Almolonga

Almolonga is a city in the highlands of western Guatemala near the city of Quetzaltenango. It has a story that needs to be told. Back in the 80s it was known as a place of violence, for witchcraft, alcoholism, poverty and oppression. One evangelical pastor began to pray for his city. His church joined him and then other churches began to pray also. There was a religion that was well known in that area called St. Simon. Almolonga was the center for this religious movement. The Mayan beliefs had been added to other religions such as Roman Catholicism in Guatemala. When the Europeans came to take over the land of the indigenous people, they brought the teachings of the Roman Catholic Church. The indigenous people were willing to give up all of their gods except one, Maximón. Maximón has been known as the god of sex, alcohol and tobacco and forms of worshiping him include chewing tobacco and spitting on a wooden mannequin that is made to represent him. This religion still exists today!

As people prayed for Almolonga, the priests of this St. Simon religion began to feel that they were losing control over the people and they eventually moved from the area. God began to move. The city began to change. People came to the Lord! People began to be diligent in working to provide for their families. Crime disappeared! The area began to supernaturally produce enormous amounts of vegetables in huge sizes. This was the same ground that before produced very little. The town jails were closed and converted to town halls or churches. There was no need for jails because there was no crime. Today Almolonga is known as the "city of churches" and they boast a 90-some percent of born again Christians. There was an entire transformation of the city!

I have prayed for this for the Jocotán and Camotán areas for years! The negative fame that Almolonga had prior to its transformation could very well be talking about Camotán and Jocotán. I want to see this same transformation in *my part of Guatemala*! I know that God wants people to come to a saving knowledge and to recognize their need for a Savior. But I also believe that God has so much more for us. *John 10:10* says that Jesus wants to give us life and life in abundance! I believe there is more than just knowing that we have eternal life and the promise to spend eternity in heaven. I believe that God is interested in our earthly lives and wants to manifest His promises and blessing to us. He wants to transform us so that our communities are totally transformed as well. There will be no crime, no lack of natural needs to provide for our families! There will be joy and true blessing to a community or an individual life that has been truly transformed by God!

Sometimes we wonder how much we can do or how much change we can bring about. This testimony of Almolonga gives me hope; to see how that transformation began to take place with the desire placed in one man's heart, to see his city changed! It wasn't easy and there was a price to pay. But it began with one man and it encourages me to know what one life consecrated to God can bring forth. I pray that my life will also bring transformation to my area where I live!

38

Gold Dust, Muteness, Floor Time and More...

I was raised in a traditional church. My first experience with *spirit-filled Christianity* was shortly after I became born-again and was invited to attend some Women's Aglow meetings. I saw things that I had never seen before. There was a freedom and an expression in the worship that I had never experienced. There were manifestations of the Holy Spirit that I did not understand; prophetic words being given, people falling out in the Spirit etc. My natural mind went on tilt and didn't know what to do with the information but there was something in my heart, something that kept drawing me back and that gave me a *knowing in my spirit* that this was real and that it was of God.

That was many years ago. I have grown in the Lord and learned so much and have had so many of my own personal experiences now. I know that people from all backgrounds will read this book and I want to share from my heart and my own experiences in a way that may help you to better understand some of the ways that the Lord chooses to make Himself manifest.

People can get hung up on the outward sign that is going on and judge it without realizing the inner work that is being done, which is really the most important. If the outward manifestation is just a moment of emotional release, then it is just that.....a moment of feeling something. But if at the same time the Holy Spirit is doing a lasting inner work that will change you forever, then that is something else all together and something worth seeking.

God works with each of us differently. He has given us different personalities, a different way that we tend to express our emotions, different preferences in our styles of worship, etc. But He can also change all of that in a moment, if He so chooses. He is looking for people who are truly seeking Him from the depths of their hearts. To the hungry heart, which searches for more of Him, He will manifest Himself and do wondrous things in that life.

I want to share just a few of the extra special experiences that I have had with the Lord and hope that it may answer a few questions for you.

<u>Baptism in the Holy Spirit and Speaking in Tongues:</u>

I have seen people who speak in tongues that are both nutty and fruity; I know that these people exist. But please don't be turned off by the misuse of God's gifts to not seek after how He desires them to be used and to miss the blessings that they can bring to your life. The gifts of the Holy Spirit are for today; there is nothing that says that they have passed away as some churches teach. I am not going to go into doctrinal teaching on each of them but encourage you to seek out, with an open heart, what the Bible really has to say about them. We have a natural tendency to form our beliefs based on what we have experienced in life. Our beliefs should be based on the Word of God. Whether I have ever been healed or not, if the Bible teaches that it is available to me, then I cannot reject it or say that I don't believe in it. Speaking in tongues is given to build us up in our faith (*Jude 1:20*). Who doesn't need to be built up? The world can wear us down and drain us and we need to be continually refilled and built back up in our faith. There are times that I don't know how to pray for someone or a situation. My natural knowledge is limited, even for situations in my own life, let alone when I am praying for others. The Bible says that when we pray in the Spirit that we pray mysteries to the Lord and that we pray His will (*1 Corinthians 14:2*). Isn't that what we all want? To have His will fulfilled in our lives? Everyone has the right and ability to experience this in their lives. The Bible says that God is not a respecter of persons (*Ephesians 6:9*); He doesn't play favorites amongst His children. The public use of tongues in a corporate meeting is something altogether different than the use of it in your private prayer life. In private use it is a tool that God gives us to keep us strong spiritually. I was afraid of it initially, feeling that it would control me instead of me choosing when I wanted to use it. I worked through those fears and misunderstandings and learned what a blessing it can be to me.

Gold Dust & Muteness:

I took a group of pastors from Jocotán to a Christian conference in the capital. Most of the pastors were from more traditional churches but some were also Pentecostal. There was a message given on the cross and the price that Jesus paid for us. It was a very simple message and certainly one that I had heard many times but it impacted me in a new way. I felt such love from the Lord and my heart was consumed and breaking to understand in a deeper way what He had done for me on the cross of Calvary. There were not words to express the gratitude that I was feeling to have a deeper spiritual understanding of what His death meant to my life today.

During the meeting I looked down at my hands. They sparkled with gold particles. I wasn't wearing something with glitter or any other natural explanation for this manifestation. I couldn't wipe it off. I felt a very special presence of the Holy Spirit and was too caught up in that to try to figure out what was going on. Do I understand it with my natural mind? Not really! Some have said that the gold is a sign of His anointing. All I know is that the manifestation came at a time when I felt very close to the presence of God and that there was a tangible heaviness of His presence hovering over me.

By the end of the meeting, I discovered that I could not speak. I literally was mute; my ability to speak had been taken from me. Do I understand that? No! I had to make signs to the pastors that I could not speak and indicate that it was God doing something. I drove all of us back to a mission house that we were staying at during the conference. I gave the pastors a wave as they entered their room and I entered mine. I had a very special time with the Lord that night. I can't say I really understand the manifestations that I experienced but I know that it was a very special time that I had in His presence. I felt like He was being jealous over me and drawing me away to have that time with Him and Him alone. The next morning I could speak. Does that make sense in the natural? Of course it doesn't. It really wasn't about the gold dust or the muteness. It was about a special experience that I had in the presence of God where He really ministered to my spiritual life, something that stayed with me.

Floor Time, Laughing, Being Drunk in the Spirit:

I attended some meetings of Richard Strader in North Carolina in 1993. It came at a time that I was very broken spiritually and hurting over some very deep wounds and rejections in my life. The invitation was given for those who wanted *the joy of the Lord* in their lives to come forward. I almost ran to the altar. When I was prayed for, I fell under the power of the Holy Spirit and wound up on the floor. Again, just know that it is real, no one is pushing you over (not to say some don't try that)! It is just a time that you cannot remain standing and a time that God wants to do something special in your life and your physical body cannot stand up to the power of God that is being manifested. I began to cry, first softly and then escalating into deep sobs that came from deep retching inside of me. My mind was reasoning that I came forward for joy and didn't understand my deep sorrow. But I knew that God was doing something, deep inside of me. He was pulling out rejection, the abandonment that I felt; the hurts that life and its hard experiences bring into our lives. Then there came a peace, when I just laid there in a time of calmness and I drank in the sense of being in His presence. After a time, there was a joy that began to bubble up deep down inside of me. It grew and grew to the point that I could not contain it. Now I do not like to draw attention to myself in a service and tend to have a lot more going on inside of me than I usually allow myself to express, especially in years gone by. But this was an experience that I forgot others that were around me, where I was, what others would think, etc. I let the joy come and it came in wave after wave. I began to laugh, to roll around the floor (yes I guess you can call me a holy roller). That lasted a long time and then another peace came. I could not get up off the floor. I was literally stuck to the floor. At times I could move my head, at times my feet but I could not move my whole body or physically get myself up from the floor. Not that I really wanted to! I knew that in whatever craziness it was being manifested, that this was God doing something very special and very deep in my life. When I finally was able to get up from the floor, almost an hour later, I could not walk straight.

I staggered and felt like I was drunk. I was, in the Spirit (*Acts 2* still happens today). Again, I know how all of this would appear to someone without the spiritual understanding. It wasn't really about the tears, the laughing, and the rolling around on the floor or the drunkenness. It was about God tearing out some very deep hurts in my life and healing me from the past and giving me a special joy to move on into the future. That was probably the strongest experience that I have had with the Lord, where I know that He did something that totally changed my life and gave me a new ability to live in His strength and power.

These special experiences have given me the strength to walk through the hard times in life that we all have. Being in the mission field and on the front lines of the Lord's work has brought some difficult challenges at times. But knowing how to trust in Him and to remember the experiences that I have had with Him have given me the courage and strength to persevere and to come out victoriously, every time! I can only say this, if you have a sincere heart that hungers after more of God in your life, you too will have special experiences that you may not understand with your natural mind but that will minister to your spiritual walk with Him in a way that is hard to express in mere words.

39

He Knows the Hairs on My Head

Matthew 10:30 says *"And even the very hairs of your head are all numbered."*

I'm so glad that God knows me, really knows me. After all, He made me this way! He gave me my personality, talents and abilities. He knows my weaknesses. He knows me in that deepest part of my heart and soul, a place where few really understand us. He knows me when I blow it and loves me anyway. He knows everything that is going on in my life. He knows my needs, every one of them. He knows my desires and my dreams!

I am so glad to have the understanding and real comprehension that He knows everything about me; the good, the bad and the ugly! And yes, He chooses to continue to love me. He is patient with me and continues to try to mold me and make me into His image. He knows that I am a work in progress! I'm not where I should be but I am not where I used to be. It is a process that He gently takes me through.

I can share everything with Him. He knows it anyway! I can share my deepest thoughts, my disappointments, my fears, my joys, my successes, everything!

It's hard to find someone that you can really open yourself up with and share what you have in your heart. If you have a spouse that is also your best friend and allows you this level of confidence and intimacy, then you are blessed indeed! If you have found a handful of people in life that you count as close friends that you can really open up and share with, then you also are blessed. But please know that there is One who knows all about you, your successes and your failures and He loves you and accepts you, just as you are! You don't have to do anything to win His approval or love! You don't have to change yourself to make yourself worthy to receive His love. You will never be loved any more by God than you are loved at this moment! Just reach out and accept what He offers you! That goes for true Christian believers as well as those who have not committed their lives to Him yet or recognize their need for Him! There is a God, the Creator of the universe; that looked upon you and loved you so much that He gave His only Son to pay a price that you could not pay for yourself. He has paved the way for you to have forgiveness and a personal relationship with Him; to know true peace and joy in your life. For those who already have committed your lives to Him, it is the knowing that He is always with us and that He will never abandon us and wants to help us to walk through this adventure that we call life.

40

Merging Cultures, Sharing Passions

A little earlier I shared a little about a connection we had with a Bible Institute in Guatemala City called CEMI, but I wanted to bring out something different here. We brought two cultures together and encouraged the Guatemalan part of that cultural partnership to be placed on the forefront of a work that was being raised up. I feel that is where they need to be. No matter how many years a foreign missionary is on the field, they will never be totally and completely immersed into their new surroundings. They will never understand all of the culture's inside beliefs or understand how some of that affects their being won over to the Gospel and seeing their lives transformed. God provided some very special relationships to be formed and allowed us to work together and accomplish much for the Kingdom of God. After 20 years I can still tell you the name of almost all of these students and have fond memories of experiences that we shared together. I have maintained contact with many of these students and have seen some go into fulltime foreign mission work, some become pastors and most maintain their Christian walk and be very active in their churches. Ana, our ministry clinic nurse, was one of those students. Working together with the nationals is an important factor to any successful missionary work. And some very special relationships can be birthed through that partnership.

41

Rated As a "Five Passenger Vehicle"

Our vehicles get a real workout as we take them over very rough terrain. There are times of the year that even 4x4 vehicles cannot get into certain areas. Although roads have improved drastically over the years this is still true today. We have often joked that we could give some good promotion to the effectiveness of some of our vehicles that successfully maneuver under such difficult circumstances.

I had a 1992 Isuzu Trooper and it was a great vehicle in the mountains. That vehicle had the power to climb telephone poles! Okay, a bit of an exaggeration but it was a great vehicle in the mountains. We were up in the village of La Puente. It is a village that is located very high in the mountains and has given many people stories to tell about our trips to get there! There were signs that it could begin to rain. I informed the team that IF it began to rain, that we had to get off of the mountain ASAP, or we would be spending the night there! There was a pickup that helped us to get the team up there too, since my Trooper was rated as only a five passenger vehicle.

A storm did come up and it began to seriously rain! We closed out the church service and walked up the hill to where our vehicles had been left, to discover that the pickup was not there.

In those days there were no cell phones and so we had no idea where our driver had gone. There were 14 people and we needed to get off that mountain so we did the only thing that we could do. We piled into my five passenger vehicle. We were stacked 2-3 high and had every window down with people sitting in the openings with just their legs inside. We made quite a sight but we got safely down the mountain, wet but safe. There is a saying in Guatemala that we joke about that says "there is always room for one more!" We came down the mountain that day in true *Guatemalan style*! We later found out that our other driver had gone to find a little house store to buy something and then fell asleep in his truck.

42

Samson's Strength?

Pastor Armando and his wife, Hortencia, my sister, Jeanne, and I had gone to the village of Pinalito to show a movie. Movies really draw people and it is an opportunity to give a good message using this type of media and the opportunity to share a little with the people afterwards. We usually had to haul a generator with us, plus lighting, the projector (that used to be a lot bigger) and all of the equipment that we needed to do such an outreach. Years ago there were few places in the mountains that had electricity, so it drew people to what was *the most exciting thing happening in the village!* It was rainy season and while we don't usually take teams up to the mountains during those wet months, we have had many experiences for our ministry workers when we have taken such trips.

We finished the movie and packed up and started down the mountain. It started to rain and since it rains almost every day during the rainy season, the ground was already saturated and it didn't take long to make the driving conditions hazardous! Before I went to the mission field, I had lived on a dirt road in a little town in Michigan called Jeddo. I often teased that living there was good preparation for moving to a third world country, as I was experienced on the slipping and sliding that either ice or mud could cause on back roads. There is no ice in Guatemala but there are definitely a lot of back roads that have a lot of clay based dirt on them that cause you to do a lot of fishtailing. Now in Michigan about the worst that can happen is that you will slide into a ditch and someone has to come pull you out. In Guatemala, you are riding along the edge of huge drop-offs in the mountains and the stakes are much higher and the dangers very real. Coming downhill is worse than going uphill because of the need to use the brakes which sends you sliding around. We were having quite a ride down the mountain, which is very stressful for the driver as well as the passengers. We decided that the passengers should get out and try to hold me and the vehicle on the road. Now when three people can literally hold a 3500 lb. vehicle on a road and actually push it sideways, against the direction of your tires, you know you are on very unstable road conditions. They may not have had the strength of Samson but with all of our prayers I am sure that we also had some angels holding us on that road that night; getting us safely down off that mountain!

43

Sister Nancy is Like a Dog

I had an interesting experience while attending a meeting hosted by another local missionary couple. John and Diana have lived in Guatemala for about 40 years, doing Bible translation work. They are accredited with translating the New Testament into the Mayan dialect of the people group called the Chortí, the Mayan group that lives in our region. They continue to work on the translation of the Old Testament. They work closely with the Chortí people and use a number of them to help with the translation work. I was attending some activity that they had with some of their people and they were introducing me to them. Their introduction started out with "Sister Nancy is like a dog". I had to laugh; I had never been introduced like that. Their explanation went on to say that I was like a dog with a bone in its mouth; that wouldn't let go of it for anything! The idea was to show the idea of persistence or tenacity, in a way that the people could understand. Although it made me laugh, I actually took that as quite a compliment. I personally believe that my *persistence and ability to not quit* is probably my biggest asset. I have always said that I don't think that I have that much to offer to the Lord. I don't consider myself a great preacher or teacher. I am not a singer or a musician. There are a lot of things that I don't consider myself to be talented in. But I am determined and persistent and that has carried me through a lot over the years. If I believe that God has put something in my heart, nothing will deter me from continuing on in that path. Through times of trial and persecution that quality has carried me through a lot and brought me out on the other side much stronger and in victory. We all have challenges that tempt us to stop, to not continue on, to give up. It is a great asset to know who you are in Christ and what He says about you and to know that your confidence can be completely placed in Him and that *nothing is impossible with God.*

44

That's My Spiritual Weapon

Back in the early years of my time in Guatemala, there was a civil war going on that lasted until a Peace Agreement was signed in 1996. Prior to that there was a strong military influence in Guatemala that included regular vehicle searches. It can be pretty daunting with all of the guns that are a part of vehicle check points. I was not raised around guns at all. My dad wasn't a hunter and I had no brothers so it was even stranger for me.

I had two young girls from Texas that had come to spend the summer with me. Bunni and Nita had come to help out and be involved in a longer term mission outreach. Nita's parents and aunt and uncle were coming to visit her. I had a little hatchback that would not hold the extra four visitors so we rented a car from someone in town and headed to the capital in two vehicles to pick them up. I told the girls that if anyone was going to be stopped, it would probably be me since I had a Michigan plate on my car. I told them that if I was pulled over that they could go just a little bit down the road and wait for me so that we weren't all detained.

Yes, I did get stopped and it was not the normal process of just wanting to see my driver's license and vehicle registration.

They wanted me to get out of the vehicle so that they could do a search. There were 12 soldiers, all with their machine guns. They made a half circle around the back of my car while they looked through the vehicle. I had an overnight bag in the back as we were planning to spend the night in the capital. They opened my suitcase and rummaged through things, including some feminine products. Even though they were factory sealed, they felt the need to open them up and search for who knows what! Then they discovered my Bible. I had an English only version with me that day so I knew they couldn't read it. At that time the majority of adults couldn't read, even in their own language. So I found it quite comical that they were flipping page after page in my Bible and not saying a word. In general these searches were to look for drugs or illegal weapons or arms. For whatever reason, the humor bubbled up in me and I made the comment (concerning the Bible), "That's my spiritual weapon, it is the only kind I carry!" A couple of the soldiers snickered. The soldier, who appeared to be in charged, remained very somber but then looked at me and said "Why don't you get out of here?" I very happily climbed back in my car and took off to find the girls who had begun to worry about me.

Nita.

Bunni

45

The Body Working Together

1 Corinthians 12:12, 18 -- "The body is a unit, though it is made up of many parts; and though all its parts are many, they form one body. So it is with Christ. But in fact God has arranged the parts in the body, every one of them, just as he wanted them to be."

I have been privileged to see this work so clearly in my life. I know that I could not be doing what I am doing, without God's help. It also has been made possible by my ministry supporters who have stood with me. God has brought some very special people across my path. Through teams coming down to Guatemala, churches where I have shared and so many other places and situations where God has chosen to connect my path with others, I have had the privilege to know so many people who have become real blessings to me. These people have made a difference in my life and in the success of the ministry. So many; have continued to have a part in my life. Some have housed me when I have done my fundraising trips. Some have taken me out for a meal. Some have given me the use of a vehicle. Some have encouraged me. Many have prayed for me. Many have given of themselves; through financial support or participating in a short term trip or ministry project. Many have gotten to know me beyond the superficial, to really know my heart. Many have stood faithfully beside me through difficult times and rejoiced with me in the times of celebration.

I want you to realize the impact that you have in a ministry when you truly come alongside and support the vision of that ministry. My gratefulness for those that God has brought across my path is difficult to put into words. God never intended us to be islands and it is so much easier to accomplish God's plan and will for your life, when others in the Body of Christ come to hold up your arms in support and to assist when possible. I pray for those that God has brought across my path. I enjoy hearing what God is doing in their lives and to stand with them in their times of need in prayer, etc. Some people I may only see once a year, some not even that; but a special bond has been formed by God that cannot be broken. It has made a strong intertwined cord that remains strong. It is how God wants His body to function.

To those that God has given me in this capacity in my life, I want to say a heartfelt thank you from the bottom of my heart. You have blessed me! You have made a lasting imprint upon my life that will stay with me. I look forward to the day when we can have unbroken fellowship in heaven and we will have the time to enjoy the relationships in fuller measure that God began here on earth.

46

Timely Prayer Vigil

I have always tried to have a good working relationship amongst the different churches working in my area. In more recent times, that may involve blessing a pastor to put one of their children into our Embrace program as a way to help them or by inviting the pastor to attend some seminar that we have held. In the early years it found voice by encouraging the churches in the area to form a ministerial association. We had monthly meetings, trying to build better relationships amongst one another. We eventually even began corporate monthly meetings where all of the churches took turns hosting a service that all of the churches were encouraged to attend. Another outreach we began was to have corporate prayer vigils.

We were having such a prayer vigil on October 31, 1998. The prayer vigil was scheduled to be an all night one, which usually means from about 8:00pm until 6:00am the next morning. Just before 1:00am the local doctor in town came to the church. He had tried to go by my house to warn me about something and upon not finding me, was able to locate me at the church. He had heard on the news that a *wall of water* was coming up the river from Honduras and was calculated to reach us by 1:30am. This was Hurricane Mitch, which brought a vast amount of devastation to Honduras and that also affected our eastern region of Guatemala.

We had 30-40 minutes to mobilize! There were some of us who had our 4x4 vehicles at the church and could readily go down to the river and begin to notify people to evacuate their houses. People had no time to gather their belongings. They left with the clothes on their backs. Fifty six homes were destroyed in Jocotán, mostly washed down the river along with appliances, furniture and other personal belongings. Many other homes were filled with water even though they remained intact. As the waters receded the people had to dig the mud out of their homes and a lot of damage was also done to their possessions. But at least they still had their homes.

Even though there was a lot of material loss, not one life was lost! I believe that was made possible because a group of believers were praying in a church at an hour that we would have normally been asleep in our beds. We were able to, in a very short time, warn and help to evacuate the people in time BEFORE that wall of water did, in fact, hit our area.

47

What God Orders – He Pays for

I have seen God's faithfulness to me over the years through His provision. I started my time on the mission field with a support base of $400 a month. That was all I had to cover the living expenses for me and my children. It was not easy! My dad taught me very well on finances; if you don't have the money then don't buy it was his policy. That training has helped me a lot over the years. We had brought pretty much the basics that we needed to live when we made that first trip by land to go live in Guatemala. Our appliances and personal belongings weren't the newest or best, but they got us through. We bought minimal furniture and just did without the rest until we could afford to buy it.

From that point to now, my ministry support base has grown to between $250,000-500,000 that I have to raise annually. It was not easy when I started, to raise that $400 that we needed for our monthly personal support. Over the years, as I began to oversee the ministry work and it began to grow, so did the needs of the ministry and so did my faith!

The Lord has taught me so much through it all. You don't go from believing for a $5.00 need up to a $10,000 need all at once. You grow in increments and you learn to believe for more.

As the Lord would show Himself faithful with one thing, it boosted my faith to believe for something even bigger. I learned that as long as I truly felt that it was something that the Lord was putting in my heart to do, that I could trust Him and believe Him for the provision to cover that need.

Sometimes we think we can figure out how the Lord is going to provide for something. Be honest, we all do it! My sister and brother-in-law gave some very serious support to the ministry for a number of years, due to a very good job that my brother-in-law had and especially to his annual bonus. Now it doesn't take all that much faith to know that your family will support you! But things changed! My brother-in-law retired, his income changed and so did his level of support obviously. It was a good lesson for me! Could God make up the difference and bring it in another way that I hadn't figured out? That year, the Lord connected me with someone via email that I had never met. This person had received a very good report concerning my work from someone who did know me. This person eventually committed to cover the cost of building our new medical clinic. That clinic project cost almost exactly what my sister and brother-in-law had been giving annually. It was something that God used to bring me up to another level of faith. Yes, He could indeed find other sources, even those unknown to me, to support what the ministry was doing. I just had to believe Him and trust Him to do what I know I have no ability to do on my own. That is the good thing, about letting something grow. Once you are in water over your head, it really doesn't matter if it is 10 feet deep or 50 feet deep. You can't touch bottom anyway and the only way to stay on top is to swim! The Lord has taught me and I know only too well that the only way that I can continue to raise the funding that is needed for such a multi-faceted and large ministry is to allow Him to bring in the provision. I go through

the open doors that are made available to me and I do my part to
share. But it is God and God alone that can touch hearts and
cause them to give and to make sure that we always have *enough*
to keep moving forward!

Photo Gallery

Early Years

Typical dress for the Mayan Chortí women.

Transportation mode.

In Panajachel.

Service along the river for baptisms.

Irma and me (a girl I almost adopted).

Irma.

The family in 1990.

Carrying block for the church construction in Oquen.

House of sticks.

Meat market.

Sharpening a machete.

They learn very young to take care of siblings.

Our ministry team in 1990.

Pastor Armando & family.

Pastor Armando's "moto".

Doing water baptisms where you can find water.

Open air meeting.

Typical dress for the Chortí

Swinging bridge to cross the river.

Making adobe blocks to build church in La Puente.

Nancy Sheldon

Moving Forward

(2000 & beyond)

48

I'm Here for the Long Haul

My original commitment to work in Guatemala was for one year. That obviously changed! Little by little my roots went down deeper. It was no longer a matter of thinking of "How much longer before I get to go home for a visit?" referring to the United States. It has gotten to a point that much more than a month visit in the United States and I am wondering how much longer before I can go home, referring to Guatemala! It was a slow change in my heart.

The biggest step that I believe spoke to the people of Guatemala about my long term commitment was the building of the ministry center. I remember talking to people and seeing that they thought that I was a little crazy, dreaming such a big dream! But I could see it in my heart. I knew the exact style of the building and could see every little detail, even before I sat down to draw the building plans.

I bought a piece of property in Camotán in 1998. It was 12 lots, each measuring approximately 30x60 feet, with overall dimensions of approximately 180x120 feet. It was a rustic piece of property, to say the least. It was a new development and I was one of the first to buy there and the very first one that actually built. There were no city utilities. There were plans for a highway to go by it but it was only in the planning stage. One corner of the property was taken down almost 20 feet, another corner backfilled 10 feet and we still wound up with a property that sits on two levels. The ministry center building actually sits on the lower level which gave us a lot of challenges in the building with water drainage, etc.

It was a work of faith. I did not have the money in the bank. I did use some of my personal inheritance money that I had received from my parents but there was so much more that was needed. We had a team from Canada that came down to help start the building of the security wall. We started there since I was in the middle of nowhere and there were no neighbors living close. Twelve Guatemalan workers worked that first year to finish the security wall and build the first floor of the ministry center which included my one bedroom apartment. Sometimes it was week by week, sometimes it got down to day by day! My foreman was a Christian and I would tell him that he needed to pray too for the funding to continue to come in. Sometimes I would let him know during the week that there were not funds to do payroll on Saturday and asked him if he was praying. We never missed a payroll but it sometimes got down to the midnight hour before it came in.

Besides my living quarters the first floor included a multi-purpose room that has been used for everything, in Spanish we call it the salon of a 1000 uses. It also had the bathrooms for teams that we would be hosting, bathrooms for the salon, a team kitchen, a laundry room and two storerooms. I moved into my apartment just before Christmas of 1999, with no electricity. I had a generator that I used for a few hours each day. We dedicated that first floor on February 2, 2000. The electricity was connected hours before the dedication. It was a very special day. Hundreds of people came to celebrate this first milestone with us. There was a very special presence of the Lord there that day. The photos that we took actually showed clouds in the salon.

It took another year to do the second floor, which included offices, two private guest rooms and two dorm rooms for mission teams. The following year brought a lot of landscaping, grass being put in, cement pads being poured. We added a palm roof covered area that we know as the *galera* where the teams love eating their meals and it again is used for many things. A pool was added in 2003. I have given a lot of classes for water aerobics there, we have had backyard swim classes, use it for water baptisms and of course the teams enjoy using it when they are here.

I am now right at the entrance to our subdivision which has really grown up and has about 40-50 houses now built. We are right alongside the main highway and we have a huge sign posted that lets everyone know who we are and what we are doing. We are just 30 minutes from the Honduras border and there are a lot of trucks, tourism busses and general traffic that goes by. People recognize the building and take note of it. It stands as a monument to the fact that the ministry is here for long term. It began with a vision in my heart but it has become a reality! More lots were bought and now we have some apartments that we rent out and a medical, dental and optical clinic. My sister and brother-in-law bought next door and they spend part of their year in Guatemala for their retirement and do ministry outreach as well.

People look at what is here now but don't usually know the story of how it came to be and what went into bringing it into existence. It started with a dream, a lot of work and a lot of prayer but it now stands as a testimony to the fact that we are here for the long haul, to make a difference!

Making the palm roof on the "galera" at the ministry center

Ministry Center

49

Making a Lasting Difference, Child by Child

Knowing the people and seeing how they live on a day to day basis really helps you to recognize their needs. It is great when we receive a donation or have a special outreach to bless the people but it is easy to see that something long term is needed to make a lasting difference. This is the reason that we began our Embrace program in 2000, which is our child sponsorship program.

There are many ways to run a sponsorship program and that is not to say that one is right or wrong or a better way to do it. Since the eastern region of Guatemala is known for its extreme poverty and high percentage of malnourished children, we decided to put the majority of the assistance toward food. It is nice to provide the cement to put in a floor over their dirt one or to give them tin for a roof. But if you have to choose between filling your children's stomachs or having a new floor, the decision is not difficult to make.

Embrace was set up to have a very personal relationship between the sponsor and the child that they support. Their monthly contribution is not put into a general fund but rather it goes directly to the support of *their child*. If they get behind in their support, it has a direct affect on that child. The children receive approximately 50 pounds of food each month that includes their basic staples but also adds things such as powdered milk and fresh fruit and vegetables; things they would normally not have access to or the resources to purchase. The children get vitamins to take and a bi-annual parasite treatment to keep them healthy. What makes a huge difference in long term change for the children is the opportunity to have a monthly meeting with each child and their parent. Instruction is given in areas such as education, health, parenting, hygiene and spiritual care. Many of these children never come down from their mountain village and coming to these monthly meetings is something very different to them at first. They start out shy and don't want to pose for their photo or go through the regiment of being weighed and measured and analyzed for their nutritional level. The first time they come into the ministry center and see the grass play area and playground equipment, they just stare and don't have any idea on how to use it. It doesn't take long to join in the action and it is fun to watch their self esteem and confidence level soar.

When we began the program only 5% of the children were enrolled in school. After a few years of encouraging them to educate their children and helping to provide the basic school supplies to help them in their studies, it was amazing at the changes we saw in this area as almost all of the children began to go to school. The ministry has a clinic that offers medical, dental and optical care and all of these services are made available to the children at no cost. Lab work is done when necessary to make sure that we are not missing any health issues and extra outside services are secured to provide physical therapy, cataract surgeries or other medical needs. Sponsors get the chance to send a shoe box; with hand-picked items that the child eagerly goes through to see what they have received. At Christmas time the sponsors are given a long list of items that can be purchased in Guatemala for their child's family ranging from blankets to dishes, hygiene products, corn grinders, hammocks, machetes, Bibles, school supplies, toys, etc. Some go home with more than others, as it is again done as to what their sponsor has sent. But no one goes home empty handed and they are fun meetings to attend.

We try to do special projects when we can to provide items such as water filters, latrines, solar radios, eco stoves etc. I think that Embrace is a unique program in that about 40% of our sponsors have had the opportunity to actually meet their child and many have made home visits to their child's home. It is one thing to read on a piece of paper how your family is living but it is a real eye opener to actually see it for yourself.

The children stay in the program for 3-5 years. We monitor them closely and make sure they are gaining weight, growing properly and improving in their overall health. We analyze the family history through how much land they own, animals that they may have to raise, income coming in through the family, etc. When we can see that the child has stabilized in their health levels or have more resources coming into the family to cover their care then we carefully consider having them graduate out of the program so that we can start the whole process over to help another child in need. It is a bittersweet time when the children leave the program. They have become a part of our Embrace family and we have grown to love the children but it is also a true success story on how the program really works. We will continue to reach out to children and see this transformation happen in their lives, one child at a time!

Embrace school packs distributed.

Embrace birthday celebration!

Embrace meeting.

Carrying the food back home.

Bags of food for the children and their families

More than food.

50

More Than I Can Imagine

Ephesians 3:20 is one of my favorite verses. It says: *"Now to him who is able to do immeasurably more than all we ask or imagine, according to his power that is at work within us…"*

This verse has made me dream big dreams. It makes me realize that it is God that puts these dreams in my heart. I can imagine a lot in my mind and to understand that God wants to do so much more than the biggest dreams that I have held in my heart; that is amazing. Even in my wildest dreams and imaginations, He wants to go so much further than that. It gives me confidence to move forward, to continue to dream big, continue to trust Him for the results and the fulfillment.

I have seen Him do so much for me. When I began my journey through missions, my understanding and level of faith was to believe for my personal support to come in each month to take care of my children's and my needs. I wasn't looking 20 years ahead or even five years ahead. God has taught me over the years how to look into the future, to continue to dream and imagine where the ministry can go. How can we reach out to more people? How can we impact more lives? What can we do to bring about lasting change? What workers and resources are needed to allow us to move forward? What new programs or outreaches should we open that can bring blessing to the people?

It has built my faith to learn to dream big! I would rather dream huge dreams and accomplish 70% of them than to not dream at all and accomplish 100%. 100% of nothing is still nothing! I don't know how many more years I have to be in the Lord's service. But I want to be found up to the end, actively pursuing what He has for me. I don't want to stand before Him one day and have Him say "Nancy, you only accomplished half of what I had for you to do!" I want to hear Him say "Well done, faithful servant, come and share your master's happiness!" I want to be found faithful to the end! Lord, give me your grace and strength to finish the race you have set before me well.

51

Child like Desire

The Bible tells us to be like children and this is a perfect illustration of what that means. It was the year 2000; I had just moved to start living at the ministry center in Camotán that was still under construction. A pastor from Jocotán came to visit me. He told me that there was a couple (about 50 years of age) that had accepted the Lord at his church in town. They had approached him about him starting a church up in the mountain village where they lived, which was called Marimba. Back then it was rare to find too many churches in the mountain villages. People come down the mountain to go to *market day* on Sunday and some take advantage of finding a church in town to attend. The pastor explained to me that he didn't have the time, resources or workers to start a work in this village and asked me if I would be interested to start with this couple and to try to raise up a work.

We started with Francisco and Alejandra. Alejandra came to me in a very child like manner and asked me, "Will you teach me to talk to God? I really want to talk to Him and I don't know how." Talk about a humbling question, one that reflects a child like heart that the Lord desires in all of us! I don't know if you will agree with my response or if I can support it scripturally. I told her that I would let her *borrow my words*, that she could repeat what she heard me praying. After all, isn't this how a small child learns, by listening and repeating? Now it was not that easy of a situation. Praying in Spanish was difficult for me anyway, being my second language, and then having someone parrot everything you say, well it wasn't easy. I had told her that I knew that she would soon have her own words to use to talk to God and that is exactly what happened. This woman loved to pray and she became the main intercessor for the church group that was being raised up. To this day, there is a special anointing for prayer in this church. We now have a church building, a pastor's house and it is an established work. When you say "let's pray" in that church, you better be specific because it is like saying "attack" to an attack dog and they are just getting warmed up after 30 minutes or so. It is the closest I have felt to having what I imagine to be an upper room experience on the day of Pentecost in this church. It isn't forced, it is heartfelt and genuine and it began with a simple request "Can you teach me to talk to God?"

Alejandra and me.

52

Does Heaven Have Crippled Angels?

I was driving down the mountain to go buy vegetables for Embrace, our children's sponsorship program. Big trucks brought these vegetables in from the other side of the country and you could buy them in bulk at much better prices directly from the drivers, if you were there when they arrived. One of my workers accompanied me. I saw a pickup stop on the opposite side of the road. I didn't think anything of it until one of his passengers that had climbed out of the back end of the pickup, darted across the highway without looking, right in my path. I had enough time to get the word "Jesus" out of my mouth before I hit that young boy. He flew off to the side and laid crumpled in a heap alongside of the road by the time I got my pickup stopped. I was devastated and panic arose in me to try to comprehend what had happened. My worker rushed out and told me that the boy was alive but unconscious. I left my worker there and went to the police station that was just up the road to report what had happened. You have to understand that people don't normally turn themselves in after an incident such as this. I was so distraught it took me awhile to speak enough to convey what had taken place. In the meantime a pickup went by; someone had picked up the boy and was taking him to the hospital. Now that the police understood that I was the driver who had hit the boy, I was not allowed to leave and was held there. A pastor's son that knew me happened by and when he learned what had happened, he told me that he would call a lawyer for the legal assistance that he was sure that I would be needing.

I was praying and crying and overwrought to think of what had happened and the condition of the boy. The police actually tried to comfort me and offered me something to eat. Food was the furthest thing from my mind. Another told me not to worry and said *that it was not a big deal*! I contemplated his words and the understanding dawned on me. He thought that this young boy, because he was an "Indian" (a derogatory term used to describe the Mayan people) was no big deal. Righteous anger came upon me and I got in his face and pointed my finger at him and told him in no uncertain terms of the value of that child in the eyes of God. He backed off and left me to fret.

When my legal counsel showed up and talked with the authorities I was allowed to go home under *house arrest*, with the understanding that I had to present myself to the local judge the following day. I sent someone down to the hospital to see how the little boy was doing. The little boy had hit his head on the hood of my truck right in front of the steering wheel. He had dented my hood and pushed back my radiator, all obviously made of strong steel, against his flesh and bone. This 11 year old boy came out of that with nothing but a small cut on his temple that had been stitched up. No one will convince me that that was not a miracle! I am convinced that an angel was present and took the blunt of that blow for that child. Maybe someday I will have the opportunity to meet that angel in heaven and find out if he left that scene of the accident with a bit of a limp.

53

Lucas... A Seed Planted!

Lucas was 17 years old and he lived in the village of Marimba. We built a church in Marimba in 2001. Lucas was one of the early converts. Lucas was dying of tuberculosis! He was down to skin and bones. Lucas' greatest desire after recently receiving the Lord into his life was to be baptized in water. He walked down the mountains for hours, in his weakened state, to make the desire become a reality when we were having baptisms done at the ministry center. When asked if he had any words to share, he said "I know that my body is sick and drying up (an expression they use to explain their extreme weight loss), but my heart has never been happier!" Lucas died shortly after his baptism. He was the only member of his family that was a Christian at that time. I have to believe that in Lucas' short time to live as a Christian, that he must have shared quite a bit with his family of his transformation and heart change. One by one, his family began to attend the church in Marimba to listen to the messages and one by one they gave their lives over to the Lord. What a wonderful testimony of a young man being used by the Lord to make a difference!

54

That Isn't My Woman

The culture up in the mountain villages has been traditionally, over the years, to just live together and not be married. Thankfully that has begun to change over time but it is still a very common lifestyle. It leaves many women to raise children alone, as a man decides to move on to greener pastures. It also has a lot to do with the low self-esteem that has been so predominant amongst the women. If a man *takes her home*, she accepts it as her lot in life so to say. Some men have stayed with their family and been faithful to them, but have just never been taught of the protection and blessing that there is in coming under the covenant of marriage before God.

It has been wonderful to see how the Holy Spirit can work in the lives of people and to bring them to a point that they want to make changes in their lives that they feel will be pleasing to the Lord. We have always tried to teach our pastors to teach the Word of God, but not in a way that puts the people under condemnation. We encourage them to allow the Holy Spirit to bring about the changes in people's lives that He wants. Sometimes this results in doing multiple weddings at the same time, as couples approach us and tell us that they want to be married.

On one such occasion there were five couples that I was to do a ceremony for. We had a visiting team from Canada at the time and we tried to make the occasion special for these couples. We had some of the youth from this team walk our brides down the aisle. Our grooms had come in from another door and waited at the front of the church for their brides to enter. In Guatemala there is a tradition of having chairs set up for the couples, as there is always a preaching that is done over and above the vows and actual marriage ceremony. We had five sets of chairs set up in the front. Some encouragement was shared about marriage and scripture read and then we got to the point of doing the vows with each couple.

The first couple went off without a hitch. When I started with the second couple, the bride informed me that she didn't have her wedding dress on! Now, we had definitely given them time to prepare and asked if everyone was ready to start the ceremony. I told the bride to go get her dress on and that I would continue on with the other couples and then come back to her and her groom. Flexibility in everything! I went on to another couple and when I began to ask the groom to repeat his vows, he said to me about the woman standing next to him. "That isn't my woman!" I asked him where *his woman* was and he indicated another woman, who was standing with one of the others grooms. The grooms had obviously gotten out of order before they had walked in and no one had said a thing, as they were paired off. I announced that there would be no changing of women and that everyone should be standing with their *right woman*! A moment of humor but thankfully we got them all committed to the right people and I'm sure that the Lord smiled down as they made their heart-felt commitments to each other, in the midst of *less than perfect logistics*!

55

They Know That I Love Them

We had invited a nurse from the local Health Department to come in one month to share with our Embrace families (child sponsorship program) about the importance of doing baby vaccinations. These services are offered without costs but so many people do not take advantage of them, out of fear or lack of understanding. Because the Embrace families come every month and are usually in the program for a number of years, it allows us to build trust with them and the ability to speak to them about a number of areas that can improve their lives. This month the focus was on protecting their children from childhood diseases and worse and the people were very polite and quietly listened as the nurse shared with her charts and statistics. When the nurse finished a few of the families addressed their questions to me and asked me if I thought that *this was something good that they should do*! I shared for a couple of minutes and gave my affirmation that this was something good to protect their children. Some were concerned that they had heard that these shots made children sick, as they had heard of children who ran fevers and other side effects that occurred after having their vaccinations. I explained that sometimes there were short-term after effects that happened after a vaccination was given but that they were not dangerous and that the long term protection was very important. The people seemed satisfied and nodded their heads, showing their understanding and agreement to now begin to do this with their children.

The nurse seemed a little disturbed and after the meeting questioned me. She asked me why the people seemed to take my words as the confirmation that they needed. She informed me that she was *the professional* and she was *a Guatemalan* and wondered why they leaned more toward my confirmation of what she had shared. I looked at her and simply said, "They know that I love them!"

Thank God that true love can cross culture, traditions, etc. and build upon a foundation of trust that has been established! People, no matter how simple and uneducated, recognize when someone really cares. The old saying is still true today that "People don't care how much you know until they know how much you care!"

56

Needles & Rocks

A school teacher came to the gate of the ministry center. She explained that all that her students had to do their work with were sewing needles that they used to scratch their letters on rocks. She asked if I could provide them with paper and pencils. I had been in the mission field for a number of years but this testimony really took me back. It showed us the need to reach out in the area of education up in the rural mountain schools. This is what birthed our *School Sponsorship Project* which provides thousands of children with packs of basic school supplies each year. We also try to give the schools some classroom resources for the teachers, since they receive almost none of this through the government. We hear so many frustrated teachers share how they have a class of 30-35 students and maybe only 2-3 children even have paper and pencils to do their work with. Then you add to it that most of these children have illiterate parents and this is the first generation to try to break that cycle of illiteracy, it is a huge problem. Children don't have the support at home because their parents are unable to help them with their assignments. Bringing the current generation to a point of literacy is a step toward breaking the cycle of deep poverty that has consumed these Mayan people and made their future quite hopeless to bring about change!

Education can be the key to change that! We are always looking for people who want to reach out in this area because we know the difference that it can make.

Here is a story that came out of this outreach to give you an idea of where the people are coming from. We were giving wall mounted pencil sharpeners to each of the schools. We actually installed them and then would have to show the teachers how to use them. As I showed a teacher how to sharpen the pencils and we had done a few, I went on to explain how to take the shaving canister off to empty it out. When I told the teacher that this was how to dump the contents, she answered me by saying, "I would never do that." I said "What do you mean?" She answered "I would never dump out those shavings. I will save them and they will be a prize for the best behaved child for the day. They can take them home to help start their evening fire to cook their supper!" That puts a whole new understanding on the level of poverty that we are dealing with and how much we can take for granted.

57

Be Nice to the Missionary

There was a Baptist pastor from Georgia that came down to Guatemala with a team for a visit. It was their first visit there, but from the time that they arrived the pastor seemed to enjoy giving me a hard time.....teasing me! After a few days I thought to myself "Okay, two can play this game bro"! I announced to the team that we were going to have a special typical dinner, using the typical foods of the local people. I explained that it would be different from what they were accustomed to, but that they needed to be careful not to offend the people in any body language or facial expressions that expressed their distaste. I laid it on pretty thick about honoring the people and what they considered to be their *special food*.

I had the buffet tables covered with sheets until the team entered into the salon where we were going to eat. I wanted to see the full effect of their reaction. When the tables were disrobed of their coverings, the main center piece was an entire pig's head. There were chicken feet hanging from the pig's ears in the form of dangly earrings. There was a cow snout and a cow tongue that was cooked and then placed coming out of the cow's snout again. There were cow hoofs, pigs' feet, chicken heads and feet. Then we came to some boring stuff like food that had been wrapped in banana leaves or corn stalks. A bowl of rice was at the end of the buffet line. The team took a long look at the tables and then turned back to gaze at me, without making any comment. They repeated this action a few times; it was priceless! I finally started laughing and told them it was a joke! Some did try some of the dishes. They really are dishes used by the people.

When I was traveling through Georgia doing a fund-raising trip, this pastor called me to tell me that he and his wife would like to take me to dinner. I thought I was really in trouble and tried to envision what his *payback* may be, but he was nice and we had a nice dinner!

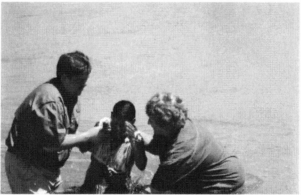

Doing water baptisms with Pastor Larry.

58

A Touch of God's Love

We have been doing short term medical teams for some time. Teams come and have their medical outreaches in the mountain communities. They always leave behind their excess meds for us to use for when needs present themselves.

In many parts of Guatemala the Mayan indigenous people take pride in their heritage, in their typical dress and traditions of their culture. If you do a study of the different Mayan groups in Guatemala, you will find that the Chortí (the group in our eastern region) have some unique characteristics about them. When the Europeans came and conquered the people's land, in the case of the Chortí, they were also placed into slavery. It has caused a generational curse of bitterness and unforgiveness to be passed down. In our part of Guatemala, there has been a distinct caste system, placing the Chortí on the bottom rung of the ladder. It has caused a shame to grow in them, as people mocked their native dialect, etc. People from the villages where only the Chortí dialect was spoken would switch to Spanish when they were in town, so as not to be ridiculed and this persecution has robbed them of the pride of their culture and heritage.

We would get report after report about someone from the villages seeking out medical assistance at public health facilities and not being treated very kindly. There unfortunately were many times that there was a distinct difference in attitude and treatment for a town person versus a Chortí person. It caused the people to not seek out medical attention. Many times they waited too long and wound up paying the consequences; for something that could have been easily treated. In the early years of my time in Guatemala, it was a common belief that a trip to the hospital was a one way trip. Unfortunately this belief was based on some truth; because the people waited too long to seek out medical attention.

God put it in my heart to take the resources that short term teams were leaving behind and make them available on an on-going basis; when the people had the need. It was the birthing of the vision to have our own clinic with one ultimate purpose; to show the love of God and treat with respect every person who would come to us. We began our medical clinic in 2004. In 2007 we added dental care. In 2012 we added optical care.

Our clinic is staffed by a nurse. Ana Orellana is known by many reading this book. She and her husband, Marco, have worked with the ministry for many years. I had known Ana for a long time and she had experience working in a medical clinic with another ministry in the capital. It gave her experience and knowledge of things that went beyond her level of study. She has gone to Bible School to be both a missionary and a pastor and that gave her the spiritual background that we were looking for. A local doctor works with her to give her consultation on questions that she has. We basically have dealt with the day to day chronic issues of the people and not gotten into more serious cases where a physician's care is necessary.

A minimal fee is charged of 10 Quetzales for a consultation (about $1.25 in value). The medicine is given with no charge. Ana's Bible always sits on her desk in her examining room. Prayer is offered and many times received. Sometimes people come in, just to talk, and it becomes just a counseling session. Patients are referred to by their names, not by numbers, as done in the public institutions. They are greeted, given time to share their needs and given quality care while also showing God's love and a general respect for the person. Even though people can receive free social medical care through the local health departments, we have found that we have 1000s of people who choose to come to us instead. I believe that this is due to two main reasons. Many times the government institutions can tell a patient what is wrong with them but do not have medicine to make a difference for the person. Most of these people from the mountain villages do not have the financial resources to be able to buy the medicine and so they go home without any hope of a change. Our handing out of the medicine and our treatment of the people are two big reasons that our clinic has had such success.

In more recent years we have received fewer donations of medicines. Pharmaceutical companies in North America do not dispense sample meds the way that they used to and so doctors no longer have these samples to donate. Airfares going up and the costs in general going up for the short term medical teams coming to Guatemala, has made it harder for them to bring the excess of medicines that they were able to bring in the past.

Due to the fact that we didn't always have the meds that we needed, we started a store in the ministry clinic. We sell clothes, hygiene products, school supplies, toys, household goods etc. I became a wholesaler and am able to buy at discounts and found companies willing to give us really good prices because they knew that the need was to cover funding for the clinic. It has been wonderful to see the favor given on both the Guatemalan side as well as donations from North Americans to keep our clinic store full. Some of our stock comes from the United States and so it is different stuff than you find in local stores and people come out of curiosity to see what we have. The Embrace children (our sponsorship program) receive a coupon on their birthday and at Christmas time. Their sponsors are also allowed to send extra financial gifts for them at times. We used to use local stores to allow the people to go spend their coupons. After the clinic started its store, the coupons were limited to being used at the clinic. It is a way for one arm of the ministry to help support another arm of the ministry and bring blessing to both. The clinic store has allowed us to buy medicine when we need it and to maintain our inventory for the meds that we commonly use.

In 2010 we started an outreach of providing baby formula to those in need. Our Embrace program only registers children four years of age and older. Many times mothers bring their babies, who are clearly in need, and we had to turn them away. This is the reason that we began this further assistance from the ministry clinic. Babies are given a month's supply of milk at a very minimal fee per pound (about $1.25). They must bring their baby back each month so that the baby can be monitored and assured that improvement is being made. We have saved countless babies from certain death as we provide this important nourishment to their weakened bodies. We also have an outreach for toddlers to give them full-cream powdered milk. This closes the gap between birth and when they are allowed to come into the Embrace program and catches their malnourishment at a very early age. Incoming teams and other ministry donors have always helped us to meet the need to have milk available. The local health department sends babies in need that they find to us because they don't have the resources to provide the milk. It has been wonderful to see these babies be brought back to a thriving state.

Our clinic is fulfilling the purpose for which it was started. That purpose is to minister to people's physical, emotional, and spiritual needs! It is helping children, who are the main age group that we reach out to, to have a positive experience as they grow comfortable receiving attention for their medical needs. I believe that each and every person that enters our clinic senses a touch of God's love and that is what it is all about.

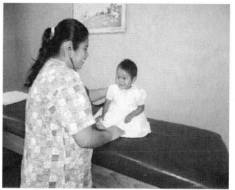

Ana enjoys the babies.

Waiting and just hanging out.

Ana giving medical consultation.

Clinic Store.

59

Give It All to Jesus

As long as we live on planet earth, there will be misunderstandings between people. None of us are perfect and we all have our flaws. Add to that our differences in personalities, personal opinions, different backgrounds and training.....it all adds up to times when we don't always see eye to eye on some things.

Perception is an amazing thing. It is the way you see something and the basis from which you form your opinions about things. For you it is reality. It is the same for someone else. They may be missing some information about the situation or not understand the bigger picture that caused you to make a decision. But from the information that they have and filtered through their own personal makeup, this is reality for them as well.

On the mission field, interpersonal conflicts are something that happens quite frequently. I know that it is not limited to the mission field but I think that it is very likely a higher percentage of times that it occurs. Why? Because you are talking about people that had the backbone and gumption to step out and take this huge step of faith in the first place. They are obviously not weak, noncommitted people. It has caused people who have come to work under someone to leave and go elsewhere at times or to look for another organization to join with. Sometimes things are worked out but sometimes it comes to a place where separation in necessary. It is usually not a one sided issue, both have contributed but the worker has gotten to a point of not being able to submit to the authority of the ministry leader.

There are Biblical examples of this and I'm glad that they are included. It shows us that things have really not changed and that on this side of heaven we will always have human conflict to deal with. Sometimes separation is necessary and both parties will do better to go their separate ways. Both parties can love God with all of their heart and want to serve Him. God loves both and has a plan and purpose to use them, for His glory.

What I want to bring out is that it is not necessary to justify your case with others and to plead your *rightness*. Unfortunately there is usually fallout and people who are affected, having been influenced with what was less than accurate information; but again recognizing that it was many times shared as true perception from someone. I personally have decided that I would rather someone misunderstand me than to get into trying to win them over to my side or position. I know that God knows my heart and ultimately that is enough.

We all will experience conflicts in life. My advice is to seek God concerning the situation, do the best you can and ultimately leave it in His hands. Be willing to humble yourself, be willing to recognize your faults or contributions to the breakdown of the relationship. Seek the Lord's guidance and do what you can to bring restoration. But also surround yourself with people who are of like mind and will lift you up and allow you to be your best for God. Pray for those who persecute you and give it to Jesus. Bless them and free yourself from any roots of bitterness that the enemy would love to form in your heart. Free yourself and others that have been part of this misunderstanding or breakdown in relationship; walk in that freedom and in the Lord's acceptance.

60

It Goes Beyond the Pills

Short term teams come down to do different types of outreaches but the medical clinics are a very special one that touches the lives of so many. The team has to cover not only their normal expenses of travel and for in-country costs but they also have to provide the medicine that they will be using. We usually see between 200-500 people per day with the team, depending on the size of the team and the amount of medical core staff available to see the patients. For each patient station, there is a need of 5-6 more team members to serve as a support staff; working in areas such as triage, moving people around, covering pharmacy, outreach to children and other miscellaneous outreaches that they develop. A lot of work is done by the teams even prior to their arrival in Guatemala. The medicine is bagged up for each patient and clearly marked with what it contains, plus directions in both Spanish and in picture form as to how to take it. A big percentage of the people that we see are illiterate and come with multiple family members and we do all that we can to make sure that they will understand how to administer proper use of what they are given.

Every person that comes through pretty much needs vitamins, some kind of pain medication and treatment for parasites. Beyond that we try to cover the need for common ailments through skin creams, antibiotics, cold/cough meds and other common meds. We use a ticket system that allows us to be prepared with sufficient staff and medicine to guarantee each person who has a ticket receives their treatment. If people come who are truly sick and do not have a ticket, they are also seen and treated. We also include a prayer station to offer prayer for the people but do not force it upon them. Our pastors support us in this outreach. We make sure that they have their medicine and any other gifts that they are to receive prior to them going to the prayer station. We want them to make heart-felt decisions and not feel obligated to go through the motions for fear of not receiving their medicine. It is important to us to make available spiritual care for those who desire it, beyond the physical assistance that is being given.

These teams do so much more than just dispense their pills. They show respect and treat and talk to each person, one on one. The extra support part of the team is able to interact and really just show the love of God in action to everyone who comes to these outreaches. The vitamins will run out, the ibuprofen will be depleted and their pains will return, but the love of God that they have been shown is a long lasting effect that they will have from their experience and interaction with the team. Sometimes these teams pick up special cases and have the ministry do follow up care as needed and even surgeries are covered financially to meet their needs. True compassion is shown and everyone is impacted; those on the giving end and on the receiving end. We are thankful for these servants who come to minister to people who have few options for their medical needs.

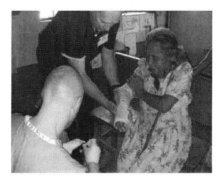

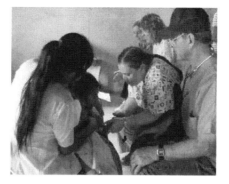

61

Saying Thank You to Jesus

Our Samaritan Project began in 2010 because someone wanted to say thank you to Jesus. Randy is a businessman that lives in Florida. Randy is a Christian and has his own factory. He was grateful to the Lord for the success that he had had in his business and wanted to do something tangible to show that thankfulness. God caused our paths to cross. The ministry had been caring for 1400 refugees for almost a year that had lost their homes due to mudslides and the burying of their town. These refugees were living in schools and churches in Jocotán and Camotán and we had been taking them weekly allotments of food staples plus blankets and other provisions.

The local mayor of Camotán, Guillermo Guerra, had given approximately 50 families a small piece of land just outside of the town. It was meant to give the people a chance for a new start. But most were unable to build. They had had to start from ground zero, having lost everything and then reestablishing themselves in a new area. Little by little they could take steps forward in securing work and the ability to care for their families but it is a long process and many didn't have the means to ever secure themselves a real house to live in.

Randy began to provide the funds to allow us to build 2-room block homes for these people. They had no water or electricity where their lots were located, so we put rain gutters on the houses; which is not usually done in Guatemala. This allowed them to not have to carry water at least during the 5-6 months of the rainy season. We gave them a down spout that caught their roof rainwater and channeled it into a laundry tub (pila) that is used for washing clothes, dishes, bathing, etc. What started as the idea of one home grew to 57 homes that were built over an almost 3-year period.

What a blessing for those 57 families! There were many testimonies of how thankful the people were for this chance to start anew. Besides the refugees we were able to help people that were living too close to the river banks and were marked as being in the flood zones and assisted them to relocate to safer places. We were also able to bless some others to have the chance to have their own homes, making those dreams become a reality.

It all began because someone wanted to say *thank you to Jesus*! Our gratefulness to the Lord for His faithfulness and provision for us should find some way to tangibly express itself. What a different world we would have if everyone found outlets to do so.

62

Persecuted, but Not Abandoned

2 Corinthians 4:8-9 "We are hard pressed on every side, but not crushed; perplexed, but not in despair; persecuted, but not abandoned; struck down, but not destroyed."

This is a Biblical passage that I can identify with. I have lived it! I left this chapter as the last for me to write because I know that it will be a hard one to relive. But it is another opportunity where I can show God's faithfulness and how He brought me through it. Due to the nature of the story I am not going to give all the details as it would not be prudent.

On June 14, 2008 a little 8-year old girl from Camotán, named Michelle, was brutally murdered. It happened in a house that was just 200 meters from our ministry clinic. There were all kinds of rumors that someone was harvesting her organs. Her body was found the following day and it had been dismembered. Michelle was from one of the founding families of Camotán and the town was in an uproar. Michelle was being raised by a single mom. She had gone to the store to get a phone card to call her father that day, since it was her birthday. She never returned home.

People wanted someone to blame, to accuse, someone to hate for this heinous crime! For whatever reason, someone in town began to put the blame on me. It made no sense at all, but it was the reality of the situation. My medical clinic was the closest medical facility to where she had been killed. I worked with children. I brought medical teams down to do medical clinics. Never mind that I did all of this to help people, certainly not to bring harm to anyone. Never mind that I had been in Dallas, Texas awaiting a return flight on the day that Michelle was killed. It later turned out very good that I had that stamp in my passport to show where I had been at the time that this took place. Before coming to the mission field, I was basically a children's pastor. I oversaw the children's ministry in my church and had been involved in working with children for years. It was the lowest possible blow that the enemy could send my way; to be placed under suspicion for such a deed against a child.

One day I was in my office working on the computer. Kim, a ministry worker, called and told me that the police were outside of the ministry compound gate. They wanted in. She pretended to not have her key and at least gave me a bit of warning by saying that she had to call me. I went down and let them in. There were 40-50 people; that included the police, soldiers and forensics. They were heavily armed. They had the entire block surrounded. I told them that they could search anything that they wanted to search. We gave them a tour, including on my sister's side of the wall where we had a store room and also our clinic facility. They questioned the medical supplies that we had which consisted of medical gloves, gauzes, etc. We explained that we had North American teams that came down to do medical clinics up in the mountain villages and that the teams would leave behind their excess meds and supplies. They did testing to both my vehicle and my sister's, searching for any evidence of blood. They were there a very long time, 3-4 hours. I tried to use the opportunity to tell them about the ministry and what we were involved in. Some were convinced that I was not involved in this crime, but the leaders of the group continued to look for evidence. They found an old bathtub that I had in a storage shed. I had installed a second bathroom, at my own expense, in the house that I had rented in Jocotán and brought it along with me when I moved to Camotán, just in case I may be able to use it. How I wish I would have left it behind. They did testing on that, similar to the vehicles. They found a substance that they were suspicious about, in very small quantity. My secretary heard them say that what they had found could have been caused by a woman having bathed in the bathtub during her menstrual cycle. They told me that they were impounding my bathtub. They wanted me to sign a document. It had grown dark and I couldn't read what it said. They told me that it was just stating that they were taking the bathtub for testing. I told them that I wanted a copy of anything that I signed. They promised me that but never fulfilled that promise. I signed the document and then later wondered what I had truly signed. The rumor circulated in town that they had found a bathtub full of blood at my place.

This was going beyond just small town gossip. I was truly being considered as a suspect in this crime. I was advised to go seek legal counsel. I had never had to have a criminal lawyer but took the recommendation of someone and went to have a consultation. Two women had been arrested concerning this case. It seems that three women had been involved in taking Michelle off of the street on that fateful day, one of them who she knew and had worked in her home. She was obviously comfortable going with her due to this. These women were being paid to abduct Michelle and turn her over to someone. The town had risen up in arms within hours of Michelle's disappearance. They blocked off the highway, searched vacant lots and passing vehicles etc. trying to find her. They somehow knew that these women had been involved in Michelle's disappearance and raised up in vigilante style. They hauled the three women to the town park. One they beat, one they burned and one they were preparing to hang. Yes, this was the 21st century! The police arrived and stopped the action. One woman died and the other two were put under arrest.

These two women went to trial and were sentenced to 50 years in prison for their part in the crime but it never came out who they were being employed by. Rumors had it that they were afraid to speak because they had their own children who they knew would be in danger. One woman testified that she was paid to turn Michelle over to *the gringa*, a term used to describe a North American woman. This put more suspicion on me. I had children run away from me on the street. It was horrible, I was devastated. I couldn't fathom that anyone on the face of the earth would believe me capable to do something against a child like this.

My lawyer told me how important it was to educate people as to what the ministry really did. Everyone knew me in town but since most of our work was done in the mountain villages, they really didn't know what we were doing exactly. The lawyer told me that we needed to take out advertisements in the local papers, radio spots and educate the public in what we were doing. Personally I had always preferred to stretch ministry dollars to buy food for children or medicine for the clinic or other ways of spending the money to help people; not doing PR to toot our horn and show the public how much good we were doing. But I was to find out that when you don't communicate this type of information, you leave people in the dark and wondering and create a place for doubt to take root as to what is the truth.

People came to my defense. People called and asked what they could do. The local mayor came to visit me personally and to beg me to ride it out and let things calm down. He recognized the good that I had brought to the community and he didn't want me to leave. A woman from a far away mountain village called on a borrowed cell phone. She told our office that she didn't have a child in the Embrace program and that she wasn't receiving any direct benefit from the ministry. But she said that the ministry had come to her village to hold medical campaigns and to help her people. She knew that I was a good person and she was willing to stand up for me. She told us that she would organize every woman in her village and that they would march where ever we felt best, to show their support of me. Letters of support came in. Petitions were signed. All of this was turned over to the lawyer.

It is hard to explain the emotional turmoil that I was experiencing. In general in Central America, North Americans are looked on favorably. We do not face persecution such as in some Muslim countries of the world, etc. We are accepted because of the assistance that we bring. I was beginning to see a different side!

I wound up paying a lot of money for my legal defense. My lawyer told me that he couldn't guarantee that he could keep me out of prison. He believed in my innocence but that wasn't ignoring the fact that the people wanted a *scapegoat*, someone to blame. He felt that I made a good candidate. The United States' FBI even got involved and came down and exhumed the remains of Michelle's body to do DNA testing. This case reached international exposure and the legal authorities felt compelled to come up with someone to call guilty.

This investigation hung over my head for three years; it was a very difficult time. One time when I was leaving to go do a fundraising trip in the United States, I got a call from the lawyer. He informed me that he thought that a warrant for my arrest would be issued that day and didn't know if I would be permitted to leave the country. I was watching over my shoulder as I walked through the airport and entered my plane. On this trip my daughter asked me that if a warrant for my arrest was issued, would I still go back to Guatemala? I told her yes, unless God told me otherwise.

I had to do some very deep soul searching through all of this. I felt like the Lord asked me some very serious questions such as:

1. Nancy, will you serve me only when things are going well?

2. Nancy, will you serve me only when people praise you and applaud your efforts?

3. Nancy, is my approval of your life enough or do you need the approval of men?

Those are not easy questions to answer and need considerable thought to be able to do so with clear understanding of the implications. But I answered all and especially the most important, that it was God and God alone, whose approval was important to me.

This meant that I had to be willing to face whatever waited for me in Guatemala and the outcome of this investigation. I had no guarantee that it wouldn't mean jail time, falling prey to the corruption of the legal system or suffering in very real ways. But in the midst of it all, I was brought back to God's call on my life and to know that my life was really in His hands. I would continue to do what He had asked me to do until He told me otherwise.

I had come to a point of feeling like the stress was consuming me. I was told that this legal investigation could be drawn out for five years and with no guarantee of the outcome. I told the Lord that I could not continue to move forward with the stress and burden that I was feeling. I told him that I couldn't put my life on the back burner for five years, being afraid of every new circumstance that would come out of this investigation. I asked Him for a grace, a special grace to move forward, and to leave these circumstances in His hands. He gave me the ability to do just that. The pressure was lifted. I could get back to being about my Father's business; reaching out to minister to people and making a difference in their lives.

The case has never been closed. The District Attorney had two attempts against his life that he was convinced were connected to this case. He had a meeting with my lawyer and encouraged him to convince me to not push for any further legal action. The belief is that this was not a single incident and part of something much bigger and the authorities did not want to confront it.

I believe that this was the hardest persecution and most difficult situation that I have faced in my Christian life. Do I feel that it was God's will for me to experience it? Absolutely not! It was the enemy trying to discourage me and get me to give up and leave! Do I believe that God used it? Absolutely! He used it to strengthen me and to teach me more of His faithfulness!

63

PGAs (Prayer Get-Aways)

In 2012 the Lord really began to put in my heart the need to get away from the day-to-day busyness of the ministry. Living at the ministry center where we have our general offices has its advantages and disadvantages. I am always in the middle of what is going on and that is good....usually! But there is always people coming to the gate and looking for me and sometimes I feel that I need a number system to line the people up that want to talk to me. It can become a bit overwhelming at times.

I felt that the Lord was telling me to get away for some special times of prayer and seeking Him. I began in October 2012 to use a hotel, about 30 minutes away, outside of Chiquimula for these special retreats. I have tried to take any Monday that I didn't have a team or other scheduled activities that would conflict and were necessary to do. It has usually averaged between 2 – 3 times per month that I have been able to get away. Check in time is at 3:00pm and check out time the next day at 1:00pm. Those 22 hours have been very special to me. The hotel even calls me and lets me know if the room is available at an earlier hour.

I have had some very precious times of prayer and worship in these times away. I encouraged ministry workers, ministry pastors as well as ministry supporters to give me special prayer requests that they wanted me to lift up in prayer and I always had a number of them to cover each time I went away. Overseeing a ministry is a responsibility that I take very seriously; especially a large one that has become multi-faceted. It requires the balance between one arm of the ministry with others and consideration as to how one affects another or can help support one another.

I felt that change was coming and that I wanted to stay fresh in what the Lord was showing that He desired for the direction of the ministry. I feel that I received guidance for myself, the ministry and others through these times of prayer. I also used this time to write this book; that has been almost completely written in its first draft at these times of PGAs. Looking out over the beauty of God's creation through the mountains and spending times of just resting in His presence has given me renewed strength, encouragement and divine direction for the future. I was afraid that it would cause me to be even further behind on what was already a very full schedule. But as I give Him the first fruit of my time, He has redeemed the rest of my time and allowed me to accomplish even more and with a peace instead of a stressed out panic mode. God is good! Take time in your life to give Him some of your quality time and see how He can use it!

Enjoying a quiet time in the Bible

The hotel

The Stable Hotel

Photo Gallery
Moving Forward

Embrace group.

Dental Outreach.

Church service in a mountain church.

Church in Guayabo, 2000.

Church Construction en Caparjá.

Marimba church.

River baptisms.

Building the church in Marimba.

Marimba (national instrument) in Antigua Guatemala.

Sunday school class in Camotán

Feeding center in La Lima

Coming in the front gate for Embrace

Nancy Sheldon

Recipes

The following are some team favorites from visiting teams that I decided to include.

Chicken Lasagna

I received this recipe from a friend, Gayl Belcher, from Texas.

Boil a whole chicken (4 lbs.) and take it off the bone.

1 stick of margarine
1 medium onions
1 small can of jalapeno peppers
2 cans of cream of chicken soup
1 small can of evaporated milk (a little less than 2/3 cup)

Sauté the onion in butter; then mix peppers, soup, milk and cook for 5 minutes.

Corn tortillas (enough to make 3 layers)
1 pound of grated mixed cheese

Dip the tortillas in the chicken broth and then break them up into quarters.

In a greased 9 x 13 dish start doing layers of tortillas, your soup mixture and the cheese; finishing with a layer of cheese.

Cover with foil and bake in oven at 350 degrees for 20 minutes or until bubbling on top. If it has been refrigerated ahead of time, then cook for 40-45 minutes.

Serves 10-12 people.

Creamy Italian Chicken

I received the recipe from my sister Jeanne Hancock who received it from her daughter Cheryl Bullister, from Michigan.

1/3 c. of water
1 envelope of Italian dressing seasoning
4 chicken breasts

Put the above ingredients into a slow cooker and cook on "low" for 2 hours.

Sauce:
1 can of cream of chicken soup
1 12 oz. can of evaporated milk
8 oz. of cream cheese
¼ c. of milk

Mix the above ingredients and add to the chicken and cook on "high" for 2 more hours.

Serves 4 people.
We have doubled and tripled this recipe in a slow cooker and it works fine.

Serve with any kind of noodles or pasta.

Breakfast Casserole

I received this recipe from friend, Gayl Belcher, from Texas.

12 eggs beaten
½ tsp. salt
¼ cup flour
1 tsp. baking powder
16 oz. cottage cheese
1 stick butter (melted)
½ lb. of cheddar cheese
½ lb. of monterey Jack cheese
1 small can of jalapeno peppers
1 small sweet pepper
A little bit of onion

Beat all ingredients together and place in a greased glass 9 x 13 baking dish. Bake at 350 degrees for 35-40 minutes, until slightly golden brown and a knife comes out clean.
Serves 10 people.

Granola

I received this recipe from my friend, Gayl Belcher, from Texas.

1 cup brown sugar
2/3 cup peanut butter
½ cup corn syrup
1 stick of melted butter
2 tsp. vanilla
3 cups oatmeal
½ cup sunflower seeds
½ cup raisins
6 Tbls. wheat germ
2 Tbls. sesame seeds
1 cup raisins
½ cup chopped almonds

Mix all the ingredients together and bake in a 9 x 13 glass baking dish at 350 degrees for 20 minutes.

Serves 10 people (but lasts good for a week for fewer people)

It's yummy and has lots of healthy stuff in it☺!

Mexican Wedding Cake

I got this recipe from my friend, Roxie Hacker, from Michigan. It is the best cake I have ever had☺!

2 cups sugar
2 cups flour
2 eggs
2 tsp. soda
20 oz. can of pineapple
1 tsp. vanilla
Walnuts (optional)

Mix everything together and put it in a greased 9 x 13 glass baking dish. Bake at 350 degrees for 45 minutes. A toothpick should come out clean.

Frosting:
8 oz. cream cheese
1 cup sugar
1 stick of softened butter
**you may substitute the 1 cup of sugar for 2 cups of powdered sugar if you prefer it a little less sweet.

Beat together well the ingredients until creamy. Spread on cooled cake.
Try it…..you'll love it☺!

Areas that Servant Ministries Has Worked in

1. Planted 14 churches: (in the areas of Camotán, Jocotan and Chiquimula)

   Camotán
   Town church
   Village of Marimba
   Village of Caparjá
   Village of Guayabo
   Village of Pinalito
   Village of Tular
   Village of Dos Quebradas

   Jocotán
   Town church
   Village of Oquen
   Village of Agua Zarca
   Village of Plan de la Arada
   Village of Tunucó Abajo
   Village of Ocumbla

   Chiquimula
   Village of La Puente

2. Bible Institute (Servants of the Master) to train national pastors.

3. Community Projects
   a. Reforestation (planting almost one million trees)
   b. Fish Ponds
   c. Water cisterns
   d. Water filters
   e. S.A.L.T. projects (Sloping Agriculture Land Technology)
   f. Vegetable gardens
   g. Raising chickens

4. Hosts 6-12 short term mission teams annually that come to do miscellaneous projects.

5. Ministry Clinic
   a. Started medical service in 2004
   b. Started dental service in 2007
   c. Started distribution of milk to babies/toddlers in 2010
   d. Started optical service in 2012

6. Embrace (Child Sponsorship Program)
   a. Provide 40-50 pounds of food monthly.
   b. Vitamins and parasite treatments, free medical, dental and optical care.
   c. Special services such as physical therapy and surgery when needed.
   d. Birthday and Christmas gifts.
   e. Instruction in various areas:
      1)   Personal Hygiene
      2)   Parenting
      3)   Importance of schooling
      4)   Spiritual care
      5)   Child vaccinations
      6)   Health talks....and more

7. School Sponsorship Project
   a. Provides basic school supplies for 1000s of children each year in the remote mountain villages.
   b. Provides classroom resources for the teachers and schools.

8. Cottage Industries
   a. Provide sewing machines and classes to use them.
   b. Teach how to make baskets and other items from pine.
   c. Teach how to make hammocks.
   d. Home stores.
   e. Improve agricultural projects.
   f. Build bread ovens.

9. Outreach in times of crisis
   a. Provide food, blankets, medicine and more to people living in temporary shelters.
   b. Rebuild homes for those who have lost everything.

Nancy Sheldon

Photo Gallery

Servant Ministries

A workers' fun day!.

Servant Ministries' Pastors

Town VBS

Town VBS

Chicken raising project

Reforestation Project.

Distributing water filters

A Before and After photo of a project the Jocotán Church did.

Cottage Industries - Sewing classes

Bible Institute - "Servants of the Master"

Bible Institute - Graduation

Lidia (office administrator

Noelia (secretary for the Embrace program)

Pastor Marcos, Ana and Samuelito

Ministry & Clinic workers

Epilogue

I hope you enjoyed reading the book and that it brought insight, encouragement, humor and challenge to your life. It has been suggested that I include some photos in the book, which are located after each section of the book plus some within the text of the stories that apply to them. I have also included some of our team favorites for recipes that people always ask me for. Please let me know your comments on the book. You can write me at nancy@servantministries.net.

Check out the ministry webpage at www.servantministries.net to see what is currently going on with Servant Ministries. If you would like to give financially to help keep the outreaches of this ministry moving forward to impact the people of eastern Guatemala, we would love for you to become part of the Servant Ministries family of supporters. Servant Ministries is a registered non-profit 501C3 in the United States and also has a Canadian office.

Please send any US contributions, made payable to "Servant Ministries" to:

Servant Ministries
P.O. Box 596073
Fort Gratiot, MI 48059-6073

Together, we can make a difference!
God Bless You!

Special thanks…

…To Myra Smith, Jim Day and Nita Leckenby for proofreading.
…To Stephen Leckenby for the book cover design.
…To Noemí (Mimi) Sinay for helping with the layout and
editing to make the final product.

Mimi Sinay